The Poldark
Cookery Book

The official BBC *Poldark* companions

The World of Poldark by Emma Marriott
Poldark: The Complete Scripts – Series One by Debbie Horsfield
Poldark: The Complete Scripts – Series Two by Debbie Horsfield
The Poldark Colouring Book

THE POLDARK NOVELS BY WINSTON GRAHAM

Ross Poldark * Demelza * Jeremy Poldark
Warleggan * The Black Moon * The Four Swans
The Angry Tide * The Stranger from the Sea
The Miller's Dance * The Loving Cup
The Twisted Sword * Bella Poldark

ALSO BY WINSTON GRAHAM

Night Journey * The Merciless Ladies
The Forgotten Story * Take My Life * Cordelia
Night Without Stars * Fortune Is a Woman
The Little Walls * The Sleeping Partner * Greek Fire
The Tumbled House * Marnie * The Grove of Eagles
After the Act * The Walking Stick
Angell, Pearl and Little God
The Japanese Girl (short stories) * Woman in the Mirror
The Green Flash * Cameo * Stephanie
Tremor * The Ugly Sister

The Spanish Armada * Poldark's Cornwall
Memoirs of a Private Man

The Poldark
Cookery Book

JEAN M. GRAHAM

Foreword by Hannah Greig

MACMILLAN

First published 1981 by Triad/Granada

This edition published 2017 by Macmillan
an imprint of Pan Macmillan
20 New Wharf Road, London N1 9RR
Associated companies throughout the world
www.panmacmillan.com

ISBN 978-1-5098-5323-6

1 3 5 7 9 8 6 4 2

A CIP catalogue record for this book is available from the British Library.

Typeset by Palimpsest Book Production Ltd, Falkirk, Stirlingshire
Printed and bound by CPI Group (UK) Ltd, Croydon, CR0 4YY

Visit **www.panmacmillan.com** to read more about all our books
and to buy them. You will also find features, author interviews and
news of any author events, and you can sign up for e-newsletters
so that you're always first to hear about our new releases.

Contents

Foreword by Hannah Greig ix

1981 Foreword by Winston Graham 1

Introduction 7

Soups 13

Fish 23

'Christmas at Trenwith 1787' 39

Meat 51

'Julia's Christening' 65

Pies 77

'Christmas at Trenwith 1790' 95

Bread and Cakes 107

'Jeremy's Christening' 123

Pasties 131

'Ralph-Allen Daniell's
Dinner Party' 143

Sauces, Chutneys and Preserves 157

'Demelza's Dinner Party
for the Bassets' 169

Puddings 181

Wines and Drinks 195

Index 210

So the dinner came off on a fine Tuesday in mid-February. Demelza had given great thought to the menu, for she knew, whatever Ross might think, that she would have to oversee the meal until the last second. She did pease soup, which could be got ready beforehand, then a boiled tongue, similarly easy, followed by a fat little turkey hen roasted, with chopped bacon, then her special raspberry jam puffs, and ended with a syllabub and mince pies . . .

From *The Four Swans*, Book Two, Chapter V. Demelza's dinner party for the Bassets is just one festive occasion among many in that great saga of eighteenth-century Cornish life, the Poldark novels. Here Jean M. Graham, the author's wife, draws deep from the well of her Cornish upbringing to show you the ingredients and recipes that go into the making of delicious, traditional and colourful Poldark cookery.

Foreword

by Hannah Greig

The opportunity to read Winston Graham's original novels closely and repeatedly has been one of my many privileges as historical consultant to the BBC's *Poldark* series. As a historian, I have been deeply impressed by Graham's knowledge of the eighteenth-century contexts in which his novels are set. The Poldark characters are fictional, but many of their experiences were drawn from real life. Graham spent long hours in careful research, later recalling his reliance on 'the manuscript, the old newspaper, the map, the out-of-print book, the contemporary travel book, the parochial history, the mining manual, the autobiography'. Behind Graham's gripping stories of romance, love, family and dynasty, are real eighteenth-century histories of death, disease, politics, poverty and crime.

Food is a good example of the impressive attention to historical detail that Graham brought to his writing. In his foreword to *The Poldark Cookery Book*, Graham tells us of his use of original historical documents to seek out information about what people ate, but also acknowledges his great debt to the technical expertise of his wife, Jean Graham – the compiler of this cookery book – who helped him to understand how the meals he mentions in the novels were actually made. And food is an important thread throughout the books. Ross's abrupt arrival home from war is marked by his interruption of a Trenwith dinner party. Later, that same dinner table – elaborately laid for a Christmas meal in 1787 – was the place where Demelza 'rivalled Elizabeth' for the first time in Ross's eyes. Here, Jean Graham provides the recipes for the roast swan, mutton, partridge pie and other delicacies served on that day at that fateful table (see pages 39–50). Throughout the novels, fine food such as sweetmeats and syllabubs (see page 180) mark out wealth and celebration, whilst references to local recipes – such as Starry-Gazy Pie made from pilchards (see page 90 for Jean Graham's recipe) – capture Cornish traditions. At the time, access to basic food, such as bread and corn, was literally a matter of life and death to the vast majority of the population. A poor harvest and an increase in food prices quickly pushed many over the line from survival to starvation. Riots over corn prices feature regularly in the Poldark novels, with Winston Graham capturing in these details the daily realities of life for ordinary people in eighteenth-century Britain.

The recent adaptation by Mammoth Screen for the BBC takes care to recreate the historical details that are so central to Graham's original novels. The simple food that we see being made by Demelza in the kitchen, or the ostentatious meals served up by George Warleggan to a house full of guests, are beautifully produced by the art department working on each series, often with the help of a specialist food designer. In her scripts, Debbie Horsfield pays close attention to which foods were in season, how much food cost, who would have had access to treats like biscuits or oranges, and who was reliant on bread alone. If you look out for the small details – the indulgences served with tea, or the kind of loaves that Prudie and Demelza are pummelling in the kitchen – you will find all sorts of clues about the characters and where the story might take us next.

To me, Winston Graham was as much a historian as he was a novelist, and a historian who can be credited with finding all kinds of buried details about the eighteenth-century past. 'I take my hat off to historical fact . . . for without it I could never have devised all the events which fill those pages,' Graham later reflected, arguing that without a deep understanding of history a writer's characters 'are simply modern people in fancy dress'. Food is one such historical detail that he recovered with particular care, ensuring his characters are true inhabitants of the eighteenth century era. Clearly it was his wife, Jean Graham, who helped furnish him with many of these details, and from her recipes it is possible to recreate the food we find in the novels. Winston Graham might have tipped his hat to historical fact, but as a historian I tip mine to him, to Jean Graham, and to this compelling recreation of eighteenth-century life. So pour yourself a glass of Mahogany (page 208) and enjoy this culinary tour through Poldark's kitchens, tables and Cornish past.

1981 Foreword

by Winston Graham

Every novelist should know and thoroughly understand what he is writing about. If in doubt he must discover enough, either by personal experiment or by close attention to what others tell him or have written, to speak with sufficient authority to convince the reader. Thus he often eventually discovers far more about the subject than he needs. It's a bit like the iceberg: the nine-tenths under water is necessary to support the one-tenth that shows.

But sometimes one's ignorance (or is it innocence?) is preserved by the existence of someone close to oneself (such as a wife) whose knowledge of a subject is such that there is no need to learn. This applies to my cooking. I have never cooked. There has always been someone at my side who could do it better and enjoyed doing it. Nor have I ever needed to inquire from others or to read about it from different sources. I am able to describe the making of bread in *The Black Moon* because my wife tells me how it is done.

Of course my wife's knowledge is relatively modern, but all through she has shown an innate flair for how cooking and serving would be approached two hundred years ago.

As to the composition of the meals in the novels – the menus if you like – this has been a sort of collaboration between her and myself and the writers of the time. Historians as such are rarely forthcoming about food: they tend to brush it aside in a couple of paragraphs. Diarists, having experienced – or suffered – it at first hand, pay it much more attention. From the original William Hickey's scathing remarks about the inns of Falmouth, to Staniforth's visit to Lord de Dunstanville at Tehidy – not to mention Boswell's; from Jenkyn's *News from Cornwall* to James Silk Buckingham's comments on his brief stay in the county, all have helped to contribute to our knowledge of the food and menus of the time. So of course does Polwhele – there are few pleasanter sentences than that in which he writes: 'Returned home to my wife and drank very agreeable tea with her sweetened with kisses.' Werner, Moritz, Simond, Dudley Rider, Christopher Wallis, the Torrington Diaries, are informative to a greater or lesser extent. And there are recipes and menus from the great houses of Cornwall – to be found in the County Records Office – which never achieved the permanence of print but are none the worse for that.

The over-all impression is of the *quantity* of food consumed. Almost everybody over-ate, and over-ate outrageously. A table plan in those days did not merely indicate where the guests were to sit, it gave precise instructions as to where each dish was to be placed, like Wellington disposing of his divisions before a battle. The expression that the table 'groaned under the weight of food' could have been literally true.

Sir Frederick Eden in his *State of the Poor* (1797) shows the other side of the picture. His recipe for Hasty Pudding is '13 ozs of oatmeal in a quart of water, salted, with a little milk or beer poured over it. This will provide a sufficient meal for two labourers.'

Sir Frederick also deplored the spread of tea-drinking among the labouring classes, observing that 'those who can't get malt liquor consume in excess the deleterious product of China.' He was not, however, an unsympathetic man, and argued, 'How can the Rich justify their exclusive property in the common heritage of mankind unless they consent in return to provide for the sustenance of the Poor, who were excluded from those common rights by the laws of the Rich, to which they were never parties?'

One of the staple dishes of the very poor in Cornwall was known as 'Sky blue and Sinkers'. For this, water was put in a three-legged crock and heated over a fire of gorse and turf until it reached boiling point. Some flour, usually barley, was mixed in a basin with scalded milk, emptied into the crock and allowed to boil for a minute or so. This was then poured into basins for the family, and sops of barley bread dropped in. These sops sank to the bottom and were the 'sinkers'. The diluted milk liquid had a blueish tinge which was the 'sky'.

It's interesting to note that when conditions improved, either generally or for a particular family, it was the ingredients which were improved, not the basic recipe. Indeed, almost up to the present day a popular dish in Cornwall, particularly at bed-time, has been 'Kettlebroth' or 'Kiddley', which consists of pieces of bread, preferably crusty, cut into large squares and put into a basin and covered with boiling water, to which is added half a cup of fresh cold milk, a big lump of butter and salt and pepper.

Perhaps of all printed commentators of the day Parson Woodforde is the most detailed as to food – not, admittedly, as to how the cook operated, but as to what appeared on his and other people's tables. James Woodforde, of course, lived in Norfolk not the West Country; but he notes painstakingly what he ate, whether it was good, and often whether it agreed with him. An example taken almost at random reads:

'I won at cards this evening 5/-. We had a very genteel Dinner and Dessert after. The first Course was Fish, a piece of rost Beef, Pork Stakes, Soup, hashed Calf's Head, a boiled Fowl and Piggs Face – Second Course was stewed Sweetbreads, a fore Quarter of Lamb rosted, Jellies, Custards, Lemon Cream, Syllabub and Blanc-mange. Desert – Oranges, Pistachio Nuts and blanched Almonds and Raisins, and preserved Cherries . . . Afterwards my Niece was not very well.'

Books on cookery were far from scarce even in those days. *The London Cook* by William Gelleroy was to be found in one or two of the great houses of Cornwall, Farley's *The London Art of Cookery* had reached its tenth edition by 1804. Verral's *The Cook's Paradise* and Mrs Glass's *Art of Cookery made plain and easy* were frequently reprinted. A book published in 1828 opens with an apology for being 'yet another cook book'.

Well, a century and a half later, this is 'yet another cook book'. I hope it may prove both useful and entertaining. But a last word. Cookery books are the sheet music of the world of food. A lot still depends on the skill and interpretation of the individual musician.

Introduction

I was born in Devon but from the ages of four to nine I spent all my holidays with my grandparents in Cornwall, and many of my recipes are of what I remember from those days. Farming had not changed greatly from the days of Ross and Demelza. The plough was pulled by two horses instead of oxen, and I well remember walking behind my cousins and getting my shoes filled with small stones and earth. Flocks of seagulls followed behind feasting on worms and grubs turned up by the plough.

Eggs and milk and cream were plentiful and were much used in cooking. Pasties, saffron cake, splits and cream are known to many, but some of the pasties sold today bear little resemblance to the ones my grandmother made.

Of course there were no such things as refrigerators or deep freezers, so food was eaten as it came into season. To me that is just as important now as it ever was and I have little liking for strawberries at Christmas.

Pickling in salt was really the only way of keeping food fresh, brisket and belly pork being the most common meats to salt.

Spring meant lamb and new potatoes with fresh mint and parsley. Spring chickens were hatched about April and were ready for the table in eight weeks' time. Hens, too, were individual: White Wyandots were good layers but 'flighty' birds; Plymouth Rock, a black and white speckled hen, were showy creatures; but the best of all for all purposes were the Rhode Island Reds – good layers, good table birds and good mothers. Sometimes the farmer's wife would sit a broody Rhode Island Red on ten duck eggs. When the eggs hatched the hen did not seem to notice any difference in her brood until they came to the farm pond, when to her horror the 'chicks' took to the water.

Elder bloomed and the flowers were picked for wine. This was not quite as potent as elderberry, which came later in the year. Sloes were plentiful – lovely to look at but sour to eat – and these too were much used for wine. Summer brought strawberries, followed by raspberries then loganberries. We did not eat pork from May until September.

This was a busy time – the corn was cut and stacked around the fields in stocks. All day long the men worked reaping and stacking; the women would come out at dinnertime with large baskets covered with white cloths. A pasty for everybody, followed by saffron buns and yeast cake, washed down with large cups of hot strong tea. There was another break about five for more tea with splits and butter and perhaps some seedy buns (carraway seeds), then the work went on until dusk. During August the blackcurrants were ready; picking them was a tedious task, but my grandfather had a great many bushes and they *all* had to be picked, topped and tailed before they were ready for jam making. A glass of blackcurrant tea with a slice of lemon was very good for a cold on the chest.

Blackberries abounded and we ate as many as we picked, but they were considered no good after 15th September because the devil had got into them – a practical superstition because by then the summer flies were working on them.

Our next treat was mushrooming. Early morning was the best time, and you could almost watch the little pink button ones growing in the dewy grass. When cooking them fresh-picked with bacon for breakfast my grandmother would drop an old silver spoon in the dish: if it became discoloured there was a bad one.

My grandmother went to her butcher once a week on market day – Thursday – usually at about 4.30 in the afternoon. There would be several sides of beef hanging up in the shop and she would inspect each one, always asking where the beef had come from. If she did not like the farm or farmer she would not buy from that carcass. Once it was chosen, the butcher would stick a skewer in the carcass with her name on it. She would also usually buy a tongue and leave this to be pickled.

All larders were on the north side of the house or farm, with stone or Delabole slate floors and shelves of slate around the walls. A large wooden table stood in the middle and hooks hung from the ceiling with smoked hams. Large earthenware jars stood around the floor to hold salt pork and occasionally a piece of salt beef brisket. What could be nicer on a cold November day than boiled beef, dumplings and carrots?

The ovens were built into the wall around the large open hearth. They were made of clay and had an iron door and were heated by being filled with large pieces of furze or gorse bushes which were then lighted: it usually took about half an hour to get the oven to its proper heat. The ashes were then raked out and in would go either bread or a dozen pasties. I do not remember ever seeing a piece of meat roasted in these particular ovens, but it was on this farm we had the famous 'fowl' pies! (*See pages 82–3.*)

Cornwall abounds now with shops selling Cornish Piskies and such things. My grandmother was pure Cornish and lived to be ninety-one. She had some superstitions, but I never heard her talk at any time in her life of fairies or 'little people'. Many of her superstitions, in fact, like the one about the blackberries, were based on sound common sense. She certainly would not cross the moors at night – because you couldn't see where the bogs were, and any cow or man who wandered into one of them could disappear without trace. She would not have blankets washed in May, because 'it washed one of the family away'. But May month is tricky anyhow; one day hot, another cold, so why change into summer clothes or discard the winter blankets? Among her less logical superstitions was to forbid the bringing of May blossom or hawthorn into the house; she would not have new shoes put on the table; she hated peacocks' feathers and would not have them near her because they had 'eyes' in them.

Altogether she was a very practical woman, with an earthiness that comes to those who never lose touch with the essentials of a simple life. She also had a great sense of propriety. Even after I was married and had had children, she still considered there were certain things I was too young to know.

All the money my grandfather made he automatically turned over to her. She had the business head, and he was happy to leave the family finances to her. Throughout her life she kept seven purses, into which she put a small amount of money every month. These were labelled in her own mind for various calls on her pocket. One was for rates, one for mortgage payments, one for repairs, one for clothing, one for masonic dues. The sixth was for doctors and the seventh for death. When she died, there was £90 in the last purse.

Soups

Nettle Soup

I went to school at a convent and I stayed for my midday meal on Thursdays. We often had nettle soup and I remember one of the nuns coming in with her hands horribly swollen after picking nettles. A penance perhaps! It was the local monasteries in the West Country that first educated people into eating such things as nettles, fennel and nasturtium seeds.

SERVES 4

450 g (1 lb) nettle tops
a few leaves of sorrel
1 onion
25 g (1 oz) butter
900 ml (1½ pints) white stock
½ teaspoon lemon juice
1 tablespoon flour
2 tablespoons cream
salt and pepper

Chop the nettle tops, the sorrel and the onion and put into a large saucepan with the butter. Cook for about 10 minutes. Then add the stock, lemon juice and some salt and pepper. Simmer until vegetables are soft. Mix flour with a little water and add to soup, stirring until the flour has thickened the soup. Strain, and stir in the cream just before serving.

Cow Heel Soup

This was chiefly used for invalids as it is nourishing and easy to digest. I remember having it cold, as a jelly, spread on toast.

SERVES 6
1 cow heel
1.75 l (3 pints) cold water
1 carrot
1 onion
1 stick of celery
1 teaspoon lemon juice
25 g (1 oz) sago
chopped parsley
salt and pepper

Clean and scald the heel. Put into a saucepan with the cold water and ½ teaspoon salt and bring to the boil. Peel and slice the vegetables and add them to the pan. Simmer for 3 hours. Strain. Add the sago and boil for a further 15 minutes. Remove the meat from the heel and cut into small pieces. Return this to the soup, then draw it off the heat and add the lemon juice, seasoning and parsley.

NOTE: The vegetables would have been served separately, probably to the non-invalid members of the family.

Oxtail Soup

SERVES 6—8

1 kg (2 lbs) oxtail
1 carrot
1 small turnip
1 onion
seasoned flour
40 g (1½ oz) butter
50 g (2 oz) ham (chopped)
2 bay leaves
sprig parsley
3 cloves
1.75 l (3 pints) cold water

FOR THICKENING
75 g (3 oz) butter
75 g (3 oz) flour

Divide the oxtail into joints. Cover with cold water. Bring to the boil and strain; then throw away the liquid. Peel and slice the vegetables. Wipe the joints, coat them in seasoned flour, and fry in butter. Add the vegetables and the chopped ham. Transfer everything to a heavy saucepan and add the herbs. Cover with 3.5 l (3 quarts) cold water, bring to the boil and simmer for 4 hours. Strain off the stock, allow it to cool, then remove the fat.

Bring 1.75 l (3 pints) of the above stock to the boil, then whisk in 75 g (3 oz) flour and 75 g (3 oz) butter, mixed together to form a paste. Stir until brown. Add the pieces of oxtail, allow to warm through and serve.

Consommé

SERVES 4

450 g (1 lb) raw beetroots
sugar
1.2 l (1 quart) stock
3 carrots
1 onion
1 stick of celery
750 g (1½ lbs) tomatoes
1 clove garlic
1 bay leaf
bouquet garni
1 egg white
sherry
7 g (¼ oz) gelatine
salt and pepper

Scrub and peel the beetroots. Slice them and sprinkle with sugar; then cook in the stock until soft. Lift them out and put on one side to use in salad if required.

Peel the carrots and onion and chop roughly with the celery and tomatoes. Crush the garlic. When the stock has cooled, add all the vegetables to it, with the spices and the beaten egg white. Bring slowly to simmering point and simmer very gently for 1 hour. Strain through a linen cloth and season to taste. Dissolve the gelatine in a little of the stock and add with the sherry before cooling.

Chill before serving.

NOTE: If you want the consommé hot, omit the gelatine.

Lentil Soup

Lentils were cheap and filling, so this soup was a popular one.

SERVES 4
300 ml (½ pint) lentils
1 small onion
900 ml (1½ pints) water or chicken stock
25 g (1 oz) butter
25 g (1 oz) flour
300 ml (½ pint) milk
salt and pepper

Soak the lentils overnight, then strain them and put into a deep pan. Peel and chop the onion and add it to the lentils with some seasoning and the water or stock. Bring to the boil and simmer until soft, then rub through a wire sieve.

Melt the butter, stir in flour, cook for a minute or two, then add the milk. When boiling, pour on the sieved lentils and re-heat. Serve.

Mrs Pendarves' Recipe
for Cressey Supe

Take fower pound of Gravey Beef and Put it in six quarts of water. Then add to the broath the fowling arbs. Two heads of Salfrey, two heads of Indy, two large Onions, a few Pasley ruts and a Bit of Lean Bacon. Chop and fry the Bacon and arbs together till brown, then add them to the Broath – and boil it togather until quite tender – then rub it through a thin Cloath with a Wooden Spoon, and then Add two or three spoonfuls of Craim.

The Pendarves were a distinguished Cornish family deriving their prosperity in the eighteenth and nineteenth centuries from the tin and copper mines around Camborne.

Fish

PILCHARD INDUSTRY

The revenue from fishing was £280,000 per annum not including St Ives, Port Isaac and the other North Coast fishing centres. The pilchards came in large numbers in July and stayed until Christmas. The largest catch recorded is that by a St Ives 'seine' which in one shot took over 5,600 hogshead or over 16 million fish. Grey mullet was also extensively fished, fishermen usually finding moonlit nights the most favourable.

History of Cornwall, edited by Thurstan Peter, 1906 edition (First edition 1854)

Rank as the pilchard may be esteemed by those who are unaccustomed to eat it, yet throughout Cornwall it is considered as the greatest delicacy; and happy is it that taste goes hand in hand with necessity in this instance, for I know not what would become of the lower classes of the people here, if they turned with disgust from an article which constitutes their chief support. It is gratifying to observe how they enjoy the only dish on which they can depend with any certainty for a sufficient meal; and though the fastidious epicure might shrink back with some abhorrence from a Cornish peasant's table, which rarely exhibits more than a dish of pilchards chopt up with raw onions and salt, diluted with cold water, eaten with the fingers, and accompanied with barley or oaten cakes; yet I confess we never contemplated these honest people round their board, blest with a good appetite, and contented with what they had, without catching the infection of hunger, and being willing to partake of their humble fare.

A Tour through Cornwall
Reverend Richard Warner, 1808

For centuries, fishing was one of the chief sources of livelihood in Cornwall, and at one time the coast abounded with active fishing villages. Mackerel, herring, cod, skate, mullet, turbot, sole, lobster, crab and oysters are among the fish caught in the rivers and seas. But in the old days, it was the pilchard that was the great provider. During the early decades of this century, the huge shoals – as described in *Ross Poldark*, see below – stopped coming, so that the pilchard 'harvests' are no longer the cause of excitement and celebration they once were.

Just why the pilchards suddenly disappeared or moved away from the Cornish coast has never been established, although I feel that the excessive fishing may have had something to do with it. If catches of 16 million fish were taken in one day, as Thurstan Peter tells us – and other sources put the figure even higher – it seems unlikely that the fish could continue to exist in such quantities for ever.

In the days when pilchards were caught in their millions, they were packed into barrels, layered with salt and exported to a number of Mediterranean countries, Italy among them. This caused an early wit to compose the rhyme:

> Here's a health to the Pope:
> May he never know sorrow
> With pilchards today
> And pilchards tomorrow.

Occasionally shoals still return to the coast, although never in the numbers of the eighteenth and nineteenth centuries. I have seen the sea shining and shimmering silver with them off Penzance and St Ives. Cornish fishermen used to call pilchards 'Fair Maids'. A favourite way of serving them was to simmer them in thin cream with potatoes.

In *Ross Poldark*, Book Three, Chapter II, Ross and Demelza went out one night in August 1787 to watch the pilchard catch:

Pilchards had come late to the coast that year. The delay had caused anxiety, for not only did the live-lihood of many people depend on the arrival of the fish but virtually in these times their existence. In the Scillies and the extreme south the trade was already in full swing, and there were always wise-acres and pessimists who were ready to predict that the shoals would miss the northern shores of the county this year and go across to Ireland instead.

A sigh of relief greeted the news that a catch had been made at St Ives, but the first shoal was not sighted off Sawle until the afternoon of the sixth of August.

A huer, watching from the cliff, as he had been watching for weeks, spotted the familiar dark red tinge far out to sea, and the cry he let out through his old tin trumpet inspirited the village. The seining boats instantly put out, seven men to each of the leading boats, four to the follower.

Towards evening it was known that both teams had made catches much above the average, and the news spread with great speed. Men working on the harvest at once downed tools and hurried to the village, followed by every free person from Grambler and many of the miners as they came off core . . .

. . . They had let down the seine net – a fine strong mesh of great lengths, with corks on the upper side and lead on the lower – some distance past the promontory and about half a mile from the shore. With this great net the seiners had enclosed about two acres of water and, they hoped, many fish. There was always the possibility, of course, that they had been wrongly directed by the man on the cliffs who alone could see the movement of the shoal, or that some flaw on the sea bed should have prevented the net from falling cleanly and so allowed the fish to slip away. But short of such accidents there was every hope of a good catch. And although in calm weather it might be possible to keep the net in position by means of grapnets for ten days or a fortnight, no one had the least intention of relying on good weather a minute longer than they had to.

And tonight there was a moon.

As low tide approached the boat known as the follower and carrying the tuck net was rowed cautiously into the enclosed area marked by the bobbing corks supporting the great stop seine. The boat was rowed round within the area while the tuck net was lowered and secured at various points. This done, they began to haul in the tuck net again.

... Ross rowed his boat close to where the master seiner was standing in his craft giving brief orders to the men who were within the circle hauling in the net. As it became clear that the net was heavy a short silence fell. In a moment or two it would be known whether the catch was a fine or a poor one, whether they had trapped a good part of the shoal or some part with fish too small for salting and export, whether by some mischance they might have caught a shoal of sprats instead, as had happened a couple of years ago. On the result of the next few minutes the prosperity of the village hung.

The only sound now was the bobble and swish of water against the fifty keels and the deep 'Yoy . . . ho! Hoy . . . ho!' chorus of the men straining to haul in the net.

Up and up came the net. The master seiner had forgotten his words of advice and stood there biting his fingers and watching the waters within the tuck net for the first sign of life.

It was not long in coming. First one of the spectators said something, then another exclaimed. Then a murmur spread round the boats and increased to what was more a shout of relief than a cheer.

The water was beginning to bubble, as if in a giant saucepan; it boiled and frothed and eddied, and then suddenly broke and disappeared and became fish. It was the miracle of Galilee enacted over again in the light of a Cornish moon.

Fish Pie

The best fish to use for this are the 'flaky' types, such as Cod or Ling. All the ingredients are cooked in advance and then assembled into the 'pie'.

———— ❧ ————

SERVES 4–6
450 g (1 lb) cooked fish
300 ml (½ pint) white sauce
900 g (2 lbs) mashed potatoes
butter
salt and pepper

Flake the cooked fish and mix it with white sauce. Season it well and put into a well-buttered ovenproof dish. Cover with the mashed potatoes. Dot a few pieces of butter on top and bake in a warm oven until brown.

Mackerel with Gooseberry Sauce

Mackerel were always plentiful, though never found in such quantities as the pilchard. You can still see mackerel for sale on many quaysides, although not strung up on a wire as I remember them – and sold for 1d each.

The gooseberry sauce in this recipe is particularly good to serve with mackerel, as the natural acidity of the fruit counteracts the oiliness of the fish. The amount here is sufficient for four.

1 mackerel per person
butter

FOR THE SAUCE
350 g (12 oz) fresh gooseberries
150 ml (¼ pint) water
4 tablespoons sugar
15 g (½ oz) butter
¼ teaspoon fennel
salt and pepper

Slit the fish down the belly and remove all of the backbone by sliding a finger underneath it down to the tail.

Lightly season. Fold over and dab dry with kitchen paper. Fry until brown, turning once.

In a saucepan bring all the sauce ingredients to the boil. Simmer gently until gooseberries are nearly burst. Put fish onto a hot dish and pour a little of the sauce over the fish. Serve the remainder separately. Garnish with parsley or watercress.

Red Mullet (and Grey Mullet)

Remove scales, fins and eyes. Wash the fish well and fry in hot fat, basting frequently.

Baked Pilchards

Wash and scale the fish. Cut off heads, split fish open and remove the gut and backbone. Pack in a pie dish and sprinkle with salt and pepper. Add 2 bay leaves and cover with a mixture of half vinegar and water. Bake in a moderate oven 180ºC (350ºF) Gas 4 for 40 minutes. Serve with bread and butter.

Fried Plaice

Wipe the fish (you can either cook it 'on the bone' or fillet it, as you prefer). Dip in seasoned flour and fry in hot fat until nicely brown. Serve plain or with a little chopped parsley or a slice of lemon.

It is a common mistake to suppose that fish is sufficiently cooked while it still shows pink near the bone. This is not so, particularly these days when the fish has usually been on ice.

Boiled Salmon

Salmon is caught in the River Tamar which divides Cornwall from Devon. Allow about 100 g (4 oz) of fish per person.

Clean and scale the fish. Put it in a saucepan and just cover with boiling water. Add a little salt, then simmer gently, allowing 10 minutes to the 500 g (1 lb). Drain well and serve with parsley or thinly sliced cucumber.

Baked Salmon

Clean and scale fish. Wrap in several pieces of well-buttered paper and put in a pie dish with a little cider. Bake at 190ºC (375ºF) Gas 5, allowing 10 minutes per 500 g (1 lb) and basting frequently with the cider.

Marinated Mackerel

Cut off the heads and split the fish down to the tail. Remove the backbone. Lay the fish (allow 1 per person) in a shallow ovenproof dish. Put a bay leaf on each fish and cover with a mixture of half vinegar and water. Allow to stand for 1 hour, then cover with greaseproof paper and bake at 150ºC (300ºF) Gas 2 until the fish are soft.

You can cook pilchards in the same way.

Skate

Skate is plentiful in some parts of Cornwall. Only the 'wings' are eaten – either hot or cold. Each wing is sufficient for 1 person.

Wash the skate wing. Put in a pan and simmer gently in sufficient salted water just to cover the fish. It is cooked when the flesh separates easily from the bone. Drain well and serve with caper sauce.

Herrings

Most recipes for mackerel can also be used for herrings. Reserve the roes and serve them on toast as a savoury. Allow 1–2 herrings per person.

FRIED

Scale and clean the herrings and remove the backbone. Dip in seasoned flour and fry in hot fat until the flesh flakes easily.

BAKED

Skin 4 fresh herrings and wipe the fillets. Place half the fillets in a greased ovenproof dish. Skin and slice 3 large tomatoes and put a layer over the fillets. Season with salt and pepper. Cover with the remaining fillets and another layer of tomatoes. Dot with dripping and bake in a moderate oven – 180ºC (350ºF) Gas 4 for 45 minutes.

Mrs Rashleigh's Recipe for Pickling Salmon

Put as much water and salt as will cover your fish, together with a sprig or two of rosemary and a bunch of sweet herbs. Add a pint of vinegar. Let your liquor boil, and then put in your fish. When the fish is boiled enough take it up and let it cool. When the fish and the liquor are both cold put in a dish with a little more vinegar and let your fish lie in it.

The Rashleighs were, and are, an old-established county family living at Fowey.

'Christmas at Trenwith 1787'

Dinner began at five and went on until seven-forty. It was a meal worthy of the age, the house and the season. Pea soup to begin, followed by a roast swan with sweet sauce; giblets, mutton steaks – a partridge pie and four snipe. The second course was a plum pudding with brandy sauce, tarts, mince pies, custards and cakes; all washed down with port wine and claret and madeira and home-brewed ale.

Ross Poldark, Book Three, Chapter IX

NOTE: see page 173 for a recipe for Pea Soup.

Roast Swan

Choose a fairly young male cygnet. Carefully pluck and draw it, then wash and dry the wing feathers and the head. Cook slowly on a spit, or roast in an oven at 200°C (400°F) Gas 6, allowing about 15 minutes to the 500 g (1 lb).

Serve with the wing feathers put back in place and a piece of blazing camphor or wick in the beak.

Sweet Sauce

4 egg yolks
100 g (4 oz) fine sugar
150 ml (¼ pint) milk
150 ml (¼ pint) cream
grated rind of 1 orange

Beat the egg yolks with the sugar, milk and cream and cook over a gentle heat. *It must not boil.* Add the grated orange rind when ready to serve.

Mutton Steaks

ALLOW 1 STEAK PER PERSON
steaks cut from boned leg of mutton
ground coriander
ground nutmeg
ground cinnamon
ground cloves
brown sugar
salt
bacon slices

Mix the spices, sugar and salt together and rub well into the steaks. Leave them in a cool place for twenty-four hours, rubbing the spices into the surface from time to time.

Rinse well in warm water and put in a deep dish. Cover with water and top with slices of bacon. Cook in a low oven 150ºC (300ºF) Gas 2 for about 4 hours.

Partridge Pie

SERVES 4
1 partridge
butter
225 g (8 oz) veal fillet
1 onion
4 hard-boiled eggs
3 rashers streaky bacon
well-flavoured stock
225 g (8 oz) flaky pastry
salt and pepper

Pluck, draw and singe the partridge. Cut it into joints and fry these in butter until they are brown. Cut the veal into thin slices and lay them on the bottom of a cloam dish. Put the partridge joints on top. Sprinkle with chopped onions, slices of hard-boiled egg and chopped bacon. Season well and pour on some good stock. Cover with flaky pastry.

Bake for 30 minutes or so at 220ºC (425ºF) Gas 7, then reduce heat to 190ºC (375ºF) Gas 5 and cook for a further 1–1½ hours. Cover with greaseproof paper or foil if the pastry browns too much.

Snipe

(eighteenth-century recipe)

SERVES 6

Take a leash (three) of snipe. These should be dressed without being drawn. Truss for roasting, skinning the head but leaving it in place. Pass the beak through the legs and body (do not use a skewer).

Dot each bird with butter and put some pieces of bacon over the breasts. Roast for 20 minutes at 220°C (425°F) Gas 7, basting frequently with the butter.

Plum Pudding

This quantity would fill four 15 cm (6-inch) pudding basins and each should serve 8–10 people.

450 g (1 lb) beef suet
450 g (1 lb) apples
450 g (1 lb) carrots
450 g (1 lb) breadcrumbs
900 g (2 lbs) seedless raisins
450 g (1 lb) sultanas
450 g (1 lb) washed and dried currants
225 g (8 oz) mixed peel
2 teaspoons mixed spice
450 g (1 lb) brown sugar
6 eggs
2 cups either whisky or brandy
2 teaspoons salt
juice of 2 lemons

Chop the suet finely. Peel the apples and chop or mince them. Peel the carrots and mince. Mix all the ingredients together and stir well.

Grease basins well and put a small piece of buttered paper in the bottom of each. Pile in the mixture and then put another piece of buttered paper on top. Cover and tie down with cloth. Put into boiling water and boil for 4 hours, taking care not to let the saucepans go dry at any time. The water should always come about two-thirds of the way up the basin, but do not let it boil into the puddings.

When you want to eat a pudding, boil again for 4 hours. Serve with brandy sauce.

Brandy Sauce

ENOUGH FOR 1 PUDDING
150 ml (¼ pint) thin cream
2 egg yolks
1 tablespoon Barbados sugar
75 ml (⅛ pint) good brandy

Mix all the ingredients together in a basin. Set the basin over a saucepan of boiling water and whisk steadily until the mixture thickens. Serve hot with plum pudding.

Mince Pies

MAKES ABOUT 18 SMALL MINCE PIES
700 g (1½ lbs) beef suet
700 g (1½ lbs) cooking apples
225 g (8 oz) raisins
900 g (2 lbs) currants
grated nutmeg
½ teaspoon grated cloves
½ teaspoon cinnamon
300 ml (½ pint) French brandy
a few pieces of orange and lemon peel
225 g (8 oz) rough puff pastry

Chop suet, apples, raisins and currants fairly fine, and mix together thoroughly with the spices, brandy and finely chopped peel. Put the mixture into stone jars and seal. It will keep for several months.

Cut out small rounds of rough puff pastry. Fill with mincemeat mixture and cover with pastry. Brush over with milk and bake in a hot oven 200ºC (400ºF) Gas 6 for 15 minutes.

NOTE: If you choose to have *meat* in your pies, add 450 g (1 lb) boiled beef, chopped small, or 2 or 3 boiled lambs' tongues.

Almond Custard

Take 600 ml (1 pint) of cream. Blanch and beat 100 g (¼ lb) of almonds fine, to 2 spoonfuls of rosewater, and sweeten to taste. Beat up the yolks of 4 eggs, stir all together over the fire, stirring one way, until it is thick. Then pour it into custard cups.

Christmas Cake

450 g (1 lb) castor sugar
450 g (1 lb) fresh butter
8 eggs
450 g (1 lb) self-raising flour
900 g (2 lbs) currants
225 g (8 oz) seedless raisins
225 g (8 oz) chopped mixed peel
110 g (4 oz) chopped blanched almonds
½ teaspoon mixed spice
150 ml (¼ pint) brandy

Cream the butter and sugar. Beat the eggs in a basin. Add the eggs to the butter and sugar, alternately with the flour. Add the fruit, peel, nuts and spice. Then stir in the brandy. Put into a well-greased tin and bake at 190ºC (375ºF) Gas 5 for approximately 5 hours. Cover with greaseproof paper or foil if the top browns too much.

Meat

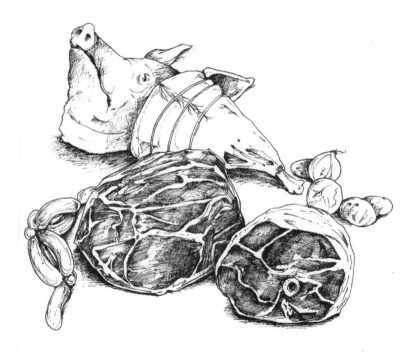

In Cornwall pork often formed the main meat of the family's diet. This was because it was not too difficult or costly to keep pigs. Unlike cows, pigs could be kept in the back garden and fed on swill – they did not need lush grazing to flourish and grow fat. We used to keep them and feed them on bran, skimmed milk and potatoes. Every now and then a man would come round and kill one, charging a few shillings to do so. We kept half for our own consumption and the other half went to the factory.

Hashed Mutton

Ross was to spend the night at the Pascoes' and was to dine with Harris Pascoe at three. He found his old friend in very good spirits. Passing through the bank with its two clerks busy with customers, they went into the dining room behind and ate alone . . .

They drank to the victory, and ate hashed mutton and a roasted goose followed by strawberries with a good French wine and a crusted port.

The Black Moon, Book One, Chapter V

Hashed mutton is a way of using left-over lamb from a roast joint. Lamb was rarely eaten in Cornwall before the days of imported New Zealand meat. Up to then it was a spring treat. Only the males were killed – the females being kept for breeding.

Have ready some gravy in which sweet herbs (rosemary and parsley) have been boiled with lemon peel, some onions, pepper and salt.

Cut the cooked mutton into thin slices and stew it in the gravy with a shallot. When the meat is warmed through add some capers.

Serve with toasted bread cut into snippets. Lay the toasted bread around the dish with the hashed mutton and gravy in the middle. Garnish with sweet pickles and horseradish.

Underground Roast

I've always known this dish as 'underground' roast – I'm not sure why, maybe because the meat is hidden under the potatoes. Any kind of meat may be used for it – steak, pork fillet, belly pork – depending how rich and extravagant you are feeling! The number of people this dish will serve obviously depends on how much meat and potatoes you use.

Slice some potatoes into a deep pie dish. Put the meat on top and cover with plenty more potatoes, sliced fairly thick. Fill two-thirds full with water and season well with salt and pepper. Dot the top with a few pieces of either beef dripping or bacon fat. Bake at 180ºC (350ºF) Gas 4 until potatoes are nicely brown and most of the water has been absorbed.

Natlings

This used to be one of the most economical dishes of all – one pig's belly, which cost 1/-, provided natlings for three months. And you got the nourishing liver and kidney included in the price. Natlings were fried and eaten at breakfast with bacon.

———— ❦ ————

Wash the entrails in cold, well-salted water (this takes all day!). Turn them inside out, using a stick or strong twig hooked in the end to pull the 'pipe' back over itself. Make sure all the slime is removed in the washing. Plait three pieces together about 30 cm (a foot) long and boil in salted water until tender. Cut into small pieces. Fry with bacon and serve very hot for breakfast. You can also stuff some of the larger 'pipes' with a mixture of minced pork, dried sage and breadcrumbs (see Hog's Pudding, page 60).

Aberdeen Sausage

450 g (1 lb) best minced steak
100 g (4 oz) fat bacon, minced
225 g (8 oz) white breadcrumbs
1 egg
salt and pepper

Mix all the ingredients together and roll into a sausage shape. Wrap in a well-floured cloth, of which the ends are then tied, and put into boiling water. Cook for one hour. Unwrap the cloth and when cold roll the sausage in brown breadcrumbs. Serve sliced, with salad and bread and butter.

My grandmother made this for Sunday supper. Best steak then cost about ten (old) pence per pound.

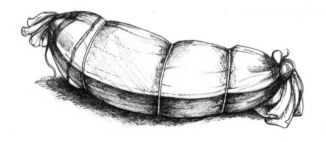

Bombay Duck

1 marrow
225 g (8 oz) cooked minced beef or lamb. Lamb is best
(Previously cooked meat may be used)
100 g (4 oz) breadcrumbs
1 egg (to bind)
1 small onion, chopped
1 tablespoon finely chopped parsley
black pepper, salt

Peel the marrow. Cut in half and remove seeds. Mix together the meat, breadcrumbs, onion, salt and pepper with the egg. If not moist enough add a little chicken stock. Fill one half of the marrow with the stuffing and place the other half on top. Cover with well buttered paper and put in a roasting tin with some small pieces of butter around. Cook in centre of oven for 1¼ hours at medium temperature.

Hog's Pudding

We used to have this at tea-time, hot or cold. Hot, it goes well with fried eggs. Prepare the entrails in the same way as for Natlings.

———— ❧ ————

SERVES 8–10
1.5 kg (3 lbs) good pork
(use fat and lean but discard all skin or gristle)
3 teaspoons finely chopped sage
450 g (1 lb) breadcrumbs
2 eggs, beaten
1 teaspoon black pepper
2 teaspoons salt

Chop or mince the pork very finely. Season it with the sage, salt and pepper, and mix well together with the breadcrumbs. Add the beaten eggs, to bind. Put the mixture into the entrail 'pipes' which have been well-cleaned in salt and water, and boil for half an hour.

Granny Trenwith's Brawn

(eighteenth-century recipe)

Clean a pig's head, and soak in brine for a few days. Wash it in clean cold water; then boil until the meat drops from the bone.

In a separate saucepan cook the pig's liver, heart and tongue until very tender.

Strain the stock in which the head was cooked, then turn this stock into that in which the remainder of the meat was cooked. Add to it 6 black peppercorns and 6 whole cloves. Boil until it is reduced to 600 ml (1 pint). Strain again; add 1 cupful of good vinegar and re-heat.

In the meantime, remove the meat from the head and chop it or put it through a mincer. Add seasoning of chopped onions or sage if desired and pepper and salt if needed.

Pack all the meat into stone crocks and pour the stock over it. Cover with a plate and weight well. Cover the whole thing with a cloth and set aside for a week before using.

Sage Stuffing

FOR VEAL OR POULTRY
225 g (8 oz) lean ham or pork
100 g (4 oz) suet
100 g (4 oz) breadcrumbs
1 tablespoon dried sage
2 teaspoons dried thyme
2 eggs
salt and pepper

Chop the ham or pork and the suet finely. Mix all the dry ingredients together. Beat the eggs and add them with the seasoning to the other ingredients and mix well. Use to stuff boned veal or poultry.

Marrow

Peel two small marrows. Cut in half length-wise and scoop out the seeds. Cut into slices, not too small. Boil in salted water until tender. To serve, toast a thick piece of bread and put it into the bottom of the serving dish. Well drain the marrow and place on top of the toast. Serve with white sauce. (Marrow is a very wet vegetable; the toast absorbs the remaining liquid.)

Gravy

People often find difficulty in making gravy from a small quantity of meat. The way to do this when – for instance – cooking lamb chops is to cook them in a very shallow oven-proof dish. I use an enamel plate. When the chops are done take them out carefully, pour off any excess fat and leave the meat juices. Sprinkle juices lightly with flour and put dish on top of stove or hob and allow flour to brown. Pour over with hot water from whatever vegetable you are cooking (potatoes, cabbage etc.). Do not stir, but shake the dish before pouring into gravy boat.

'Julia's Christening'

The second christening party went off without a hitch . . . This was a summer feast in the old style, with no new-fangled dainties to embarrass anyone. Demelza and Verity and Prudie had been working on it from early morning. Huge beef pies had been made; repeated layers of pastry and beef laid on top of each other in great dishes with cream poured over. Four green geese and twelve fine capons had been roasted; cakes made as big as millstones. There was bee wine and home-brewed ale and cider and port. Ross had reckoned on five quarts of cider for each man and three for each woman, and he thought that this would be just enough.

. . . Then, having worked off some of their dinner, they were all invited in again to drink tea and eat heavy cake and saffron cake and gingerbreads.

Demelza, Book One, Chapter V

Beef Pie

SERVES 6

900 g (2 lbs) stewing or chuck steak
100 g (4 oz) beef fat
seasoned flour
225 g (8 oz) ox kidney
1 medium-sized onion
salt and pepper
225 g (8 oz) flaky pastry

Cut the meat into thin slices. Put a small piece of fat on the meat and roll up. (The fat helps to tenderize the meat.) Roll in seasoned flour and put into a deep pie dish. Chop the kidney and onion and add to the meat. Cover with cold water. Put into a hot oven – 200°C (400°F) Gas 6 – bring to the boil, and turn down heat to 150°C (300°F) Gas 2 and allow to simmer for 3 hours, adding more water during cooking if necessary.

Remove from oven, allow the dish to cool and then cover with pastry. Cook at 225°C (425°F) Gas 7 until nicely brown (about 20 minutes).

Roast Green Goose

SERVES 8
1 goose
fresh sage and thyme
1 onion
450 g (1 lb) fine white breadcrumbs
2 eggs, beaten
salt and pepper

Choose a nice young hen bird, weighing about 4½ kg (10 lbs), if possible. A green goose, in fact, is a very young goose, as against a fully-grown one, which is usually eaten at Christmas.

Put the herbs in the oven to dry for about 20 minutes. Strip the leaves from the stalks and crush them with a rolling pin. Peel and chop the onion and boil it until soft. Drain, and mix with the herbs and breadcrumbs. Season well and bind the mixture with the beaten eggs. Stuff the goose with this mixture. Then sprinkle the breast with salt and roast it at 200ºC (400ºF) Gas 6, allowing about 15 minutes to the 500 g (1 lb) and 15 minutes over. (It is cooked when the drumsticks are tender.) Baste frequently during cooking with the fat that comes from the bird.

Take about 225 g (8 oz) melted butter. Add a spoonful of chopped sorrel, a little sugar and about 225 g (8 oz) gooseberries. Simmer all together gently and serve hot with the goose.

Capon

A 3 KG (7 LB) BIRD SERVES ABOUT 6 PEOPLE

Wipe the inside of the bird with a damp cloth, and stuff with parsley stuffing. Stuff the neck part as well.

Smear the breast with butter and salt and roast in a hot oven – 200°C (400°F) Gas 6 – allowing 20 minutes to the 500 g (1 lb) and 20 minutes over. Baste the bird frequently. About half an hour before cooking is complete, put 6 or 8 rashers of bacon over the breast.

Christening Cake

225 g (8 oz) butter
225 g (8 oz) soft brown sugar
5 eggs
275 g (10 oz) self-raising flour
¼ teaspoon salt
1 level teaspoon mixed spice
½ teaspoon ground ginger
2 teaspoons rum
1 teaspoon almond essence
225 g (8 oz) currants
225 g (8 oz) sultanas
25 g (1 oz) mixed peel
25 g (1 oz) chopped glacé cherries
225 g (8 oz) ground almonds
25 g (1 oz) blanched chopped almonds

Line a 20 cm (8-inch) cake tin with buttered greaseproof paper. Cream the butter and sugar together thoroughly. Beat the eggs and add alternately with the flour, salt and mixed spices (mixed together). Add rum and almond essence, stirring or folding it in, not beating. Finally, stir in all the dried fruits and nuts.

Put into the prepared cake tin and bake in the middle of the oven at 170ºC (325ºF) Gas 3 for 1 hour. Reduce temperature to 145ºC (290ºF) Gas 1½ and cook for a further 2 hours. Remove from oven and leave in tin until cool. Store for 3 weeks then cover with almond paste and royal icing.

Heavy Cake

450 g (1 lb) flour
100 g (4 oz) butter
50 g (2 oz) lard
175 g (6 oz) sugar
350 g (12 oz) currants
pinch of salt
2 eggs, beaten
300 ml (½ pint) milk

Sift the flour and rub the fat into it. Add sugar, currants
and a pinch of salt. Mix the beaten eggs with the milk
and add to the mixture (reserve a few spoonfuls) to make
a soft dough. Turn onto a well-floured board and roll
out to a thickness of about 1.5 cm (¾ inch). Put on to
a baking sheet and score the top into a lattice pattern.
Brush over with egg and milk and bake for 30 minutes
at 200ºC (400ºF) Gas 6.

Saffron Cake

1 g (½ dram) saffron
900 g (2 lbs) plain flour
450 g (1 lb) butter
pinch of salt
100 g (4 oz) sugar
50 g (2 oz) candied peel, chopped
450 g (1 lb) currants
25 g (1 oz) yeast
warm milk
sugar

Put the saffron in a basin and cover with boiling water. Leave overnight to soak. Sift the flour and rub the butter into it. Add salt, sugar, chopped peel and currants. Put the yeast into a cup, mix with a little warm milk and add a spoonful of sugar. Make a small well in the centre of the flour and pour the yeast into it. Sprinkle with flour and leave until the yeast begins to bubble and break through. Mix by hand with some more warm milk and strained saffron into a firm dough. Leave in a warm place to rise. Put into a well-greased cake tin and bake for 1 hour at 180ºC (350ºF) Gas 4.

Gingerbread

225 g (8 oz) butter
100 g (4 oz) brown sugar
225 g (8 oz) black treacle
6 eggs
2 teaspoons bicarbonate of soda
450 g (1 lb) flour and oatmeal, mixed
¼ teaspoon salt
4 teaspoons ginger
1 teaspoon cinnamon
a little milk to mix

Cream the butter, sugar and treacle and beat in the eggs. Add the bicarbonate of soda, flour and oatmeal, salt, ginger and cinnamon. Add sufficient milk to make a mixture which can be rolled out.

Roll out to a thickness of 5 mm (¼ inch) and cut into rounds. Bake in a moderate oven 180ºC (350ºF) Gas 4 for 23 minutes.

Bee Wine

Bee wine was so called because of the appearance of the yeast working up and down in the jar. It forms fluffy lumps which look not unlike bumble bees. This old recipe was also called the '*Balm of Giliad*'.

———— ❧ ————

Dissolve 50 g (2 oz) demerara sugar in 600 ml (1 pint) cold water in a glass jar. Add about 50 g (2 oz) brewer's yeast and put in a warm place, covered with muslin. Add 1 teaspoon ground ginger and 1 teaspoon demerara sugar every day for a week.

Dissolve 3½ tea cups of sugar in 4 tea cups of boiling water and make up to 2.75 l (5 pints) with cold water. Add the juice of 1 large lemon.

Strain the yeast mixture into the syrup and bottle the wine in strong bottles. Leave for a few hours, then screw the tops down tightly. The wine is ready to drink in 4 weeks and the sediment at the bottom of the bottles may be used for the next lot of wine.

Pies

It is said that the Devil will not come into Cornwall for fear of being cut up and put into a pye. The people of Cornwall make pyes of almost anything eatable, and thus render many things not eatable, except to themselves: witness their squab-pye, sweet-giblet pye, herby pye, muggetty pye, etc.

Richard Polwhele, *History of Cornwall*, 1803

Richard Polwhele's words echo occasionally through the Poldark books – witness *Demelza*, Book Two, Chapter III:

'It rained all night, but by eight the day was clearing and a fresh soft wind blew from the south-west. Mark Daniel had spent his whole morning in the garden, but at half an hour after noon he came in to eat his dinner and get ready for the mine. Karen had made a herb pie out of things she had been able to gather and had flavoured it with two rabbit legs she had bought from Mrs Vigus.'

Pies, tarts and tartlets of all sorts were regular fare at both Nampara and Trenwith. Again in *Demelza* we are told how Mr Odgers, when dining one evening with Frances and Elizabeth at Trenwith, waited 'impatiently until he too could sit down and begin on the cold fowl and the gooseberry pies'.

Towards the end of that book, when Ross returned home late one night, Demelza tells him 'I've saved some pie for you. Or there's cold chicken if you want. And some nice fresh cakes and tarts'.

In *The Black Moon* at a late supper at Nampara, Ross tells Demelza he will only eat the gooseberry tart if she had made it.

Conger Eel Pie

My grandfather and uncle used to go fishing for conger eels. They are still caught off the Cornish coast.

———— ❧ ————

SERVES 4–6
1 small conger eel
2 teaspoons chopped parsley
225 g (8 oz) rough puff pastry (see page 141)
salt and pepper

Wash and dry the fish. Remove all bone and cut the flesh into small pieces. Put in a pie dish. Season well and add parsley. Add enough water to cover fish and cover with rolled-out pastry. Cook in hot oven 200°C (400°F) Gas 6 to set pastry and then lower the temperature to 180°C (350°F) Gas 4. Cook for about 1 hour in all.

Fowl Pie

Some of my cousins lived in North Cornwall not far from Roscarrack, the farm used for the original television film of Nampara. They were Methodists and it was the custom every so often to invite the local preacher to Sunday dinner. On one occasion when I was staying on the farm, my aunt decided to have boiled fowl. Two or three large birds were killed and plucked the day before and cooked over an open fire in an enormous iron saucepan. There was also a large piece of belly pork and mountains of potatoes and greens. We sat down to dinner – fourteen or fifteen of us – at a long kitchen table. I was just about to start mine when I heard one of my cousins say, 'Preacher Fowle will say grace first.' I was about five years old at the time, very plump, with an uncontrollable giggle. I started to laugh and could not stop. The others saw nothing funny in the connection. I was not popular for quite a while.

SERVES 8
1 large fowl, weighing about 3 kg (7 lbs)
3 hard-boiled eggs
1 tablespoon parsley
275 g (10 oz) short crust pastry (see page 155)
salt and pepper

Boil the fowl in slightly salted water until it is tender. Cut into joints and skin them. Put into an ovenproof pie dish and cover with the sliced hard-boiled eggs. Sprinkle with chopped parsley. Season and half fill with stock in which the fowl was boiled. Cover with a pastry lid and bake at 200°C (400°F) Gas 6 until the pastry is brown.

> Round the dining table of the parlour of Nampara House one windy afternoon in 1787 six gentlemen were seated.
>
> They had dined and wined well, off part of a large cod, a chine of mutton, a chicken pie, some pigeons and a fillet of veal with roasted sweetbreads, apricot tart, a dish of cream and almonds and raisins.
>
> *Ross Poldark*, Book Two, Chapter I

At my cousins' farm, the chicken or fowl would be killed and brought in complete with feathers. It was then plucked and singed. The feathers except the wing feathers were put in a bag and put in a warm oven to kill all the mites. These feathers were kept until there were sufficient to make a pillow. The nails were cut off and the feet put in a basin of boiling water and then skinned. These were then added to the gizzard (already emptied and skinned), the liver and heart. All these were boiled together to make stock for gravy.

Pigeons

Pigeons are in season all the year round and, properly cooked, are exceptionally good. Allow half a pigeon per person.

———— ꧁ ————

3 pigeons
1 egg
3 tablespoons thick cream
1 dessertspoon butter
thyme
mace
parsley

To stew a pigeon: Take pigeons with their giblets and cut them in quarters. Put them in stew pan with two blades of mace, salt and pepper. Put just enough water to stew them without burning. When they are tender strain off the liquid and reserve. Beat together the yolk of the egg, the cream, the butter and chopped thyme and parsley. Stir into the hot stock from the pigeon. Do not allow to boil or it will curdle. Pour over pigeons.

Lamb Tail Pie

It is the custom to cut the lambs' tails off a few days after birth, as sheep are very prone to ticks, and docking the tail keeps the lamb much cleaner. The practice now is to tie a nylon thread around the tail which stops the circulation and the tails drop off. In earlier days, however, a farmer would have just as many cut per day as he needed for his supper, as the tails are very succulent and tender.

SERVES 4—6
8 lambs' tails
1 tablespoon chopped parsley
225 g (8 oz) rough puff pastry (see page 141)
salt and pepper
sprigs mint

Wash the lambs' tails in hot water and pull off the wool. Then wash them thoroughly again in cold water. Cut into pieces at the joints and put these into a pie dish with the chopped parsley and some salt and pepper. Cover with water. Roll out the puff pastry and cover the dish with it. Bake at 200ºC (400ºF) Gas 6 for half an hour. Serve with sprigs of mint and new potatoes.

Meat and Potato Pie

This was sometimes known as '100–1' meaning 100 pieces of potato to 1 piece of meat.

———————— ✦ ————————

SERVES 4–6

6 large floury potatoes
225 g (8 oz) steak
1 onion
225 g (8 oz) short crust pastry (see page 155)
salt and pepper

Slice the potatoes finely into a pie dish or ovenproof dish. Dot with pieces of meat and chopped onion. Season well and half fill with cold water. Cover with a plate (or foil) and put into oven at 200ºC (400ºF) Gas 6 until the water is boiling. Simmer for 45 minutes. Cover with short crust pastry and bake until the pastry is well browned.

Egg and Bacon Pie

SERVES 6

275 g (10 oz) short crust pastry (see page 155)
6 slices smoked bacon
3 eggs
salt and pepper

Line a shallow enamel plate with half the pastry. Cut the bacon into pieces and scatter it over the pastry. Break the eggs carefully on to the bacon; season well and cover with a pastry lid. Bake in a hot oven – 200°C (400°F) Gas 6 – until pastry is nicely browned – about 25 minutes.

Fried Patties
(circa 1783)

Mince a bit of cold veal and six oysters. Mix with a few crumbs of bread, salt, pepper, nutmeg, and a very small bit of lemon peel. Add the liquor of the oysters. Warm all, but do not boil. Let it go cold. Have ready a good puff paste, roll thin, and cut it in round or square bits. Put some of the above mixture between two of these bits and twist the edges. Fry them a fine brown.

This is a very good thing, and baked, is a very fashionable dish. Brush all the patties over with egg before baking.

In the eighteenth century oysters were plentiful in the Truro river and sold at 3d a hundred. Great quantities were shipped overseas in quart barrels made of split withies. Much of the trade was with the West Indies.

Squab Pie

'Squab' Pie, in its various permutations, has been popular fare all over the West Country for centuries. Sometimes it contains pigeons, sometimes it is made with lamb or mutton instead of veal, but it always contains apples.

The origins of the name are a little hazy – it could stem from a mispronunciation. This recipe is an old version of the dish.

SERVES 4

Cut 450 g (1 lb) of veal into slices. Line a pie dish with some of the meat and cover with sliced apples. Sprinkle with sugar. Add slices of onion, a handful of currants and sultanas and a little mixed spice and continue layering until dish is full. Add some good meat stock. Cover with pastry and cook for 1 hour at 190°C (375°F) Gas 5.

Starry-Gazy Pie

A rarity nowadays, but often made in the past, usually with pilchards. The name is obvious from its appearance, for the fish heads stare up at you from the middle of the pie crust. This is another dish with endless variations. Sometimes chopped herbs and spices were used to stuff the fish; sometimes chopped onions and bacon were added together with beaten eggs and cream.

The following version is how I remember it.

Allow 2 fish to each person (if the fish are fairly small). You could alternatively use pilchards, mackerel or herrings.

Clean the fish well, remove all scales and the backbone but leave the heads in place. Boil 2 eggs until they are hard; then slice them. Grease a pie dish and put the fish in it with the heads towards the middle. Add the eggs and salt and pepper. Cover with flaky pastry and make a slit for the heads to come through. Bake in a moderate oven until the pastry is brown and the fish cooked.

There is a story that a stranger from 'up-country' was once eating a starry-gazy pie and he complained that the fish's backbone was exceptionally hard. 'Let me see, my dear!' cried the woman, coming forward to the table, 'Why that edn' no fish bone at all. That's our little Johnny's hair comb, what he lost two days ago – careless little emp!'

Giblet Pie

We used to use up the giblets from the Christmas turkey or goose in this pie. The liver, gizzard and heart all went into it.

———— ∿ ————

SERVES ABOUT 4 PEOPLE

Wash the giblets well in salted water, then cut them up fairly coarsely. Put in a pie dish with 2 hard-boiled eggs and some finely chopped parsley and cover with chicken stock. Season well. Cover with rough puff pastry and cook for 1 hour at 190ºC (375ºF) Gas 5.

Mincemeat for Pies

There is an alternative recipe for mincemeat on page 49. It will make 8–10 jarfuls (450 g/1 lb size) and keeps for 2–3 months.

————— ❧ —————

1.5 kg (3 lbs) suet
900 g (2 lbs) raisins
900 g (2 lbs) currants
50 small apples
225 g (8 oz) castor sugar
7 g (¼ oz) mace
7 g (¼ oz) cloves
2 small nutmegs
300 ml (½ pint) brandy
300 ml (½ pint) sack (light wine)

Finely chop the suet; stone and finely chop the raisins and wash and dry the currants. Peel, core and chop the apples. Pound together the sugar and spices until they are finely crushed and well mixed. Put all these ingredients together in a large (not metal) container and stir in the brandy and wine. Keep tightly covered until wanted.

To make pies: put a thin layer of puff pastry in the bottom of a dish, then a thin layer of the mincemeat, a thin layer of lemon peel and another layer of mincemeat.

Top this with a thin layer of orange peel, the juice of half a Seville orange or lemon and 3 tablespoons of red wine. Cover with thin pastry and bake in a moderate oven until the pastry is cooked.

'Christmas at Trenwith 1790'

It wasn't the sort of meal they'd had before, either, though it was the best put on for two years. They had ham and fowls and a leg of mutton, boiled, with caper sauce, and afterwards batter pudding and currant jelly and damson tarts and black caps in custard, and blancmange.

Jeremy Poldark, Book Two, Chapter III

Ham

Boil a large ham with 2 large onions, allowing 25 minutes to the 500g (1 lb) and 25 minutes over. Remove from the water and skin. Stick well with cloves, pressing them hard into the fat. Then cover with brown sugar and put into a deep baking dish. Pour 1.2l (2 pints) of cider around the ham and bake in a hot oven – 200ºC (400ºF) Gas 6 – until the sugar is nicely browned.

Fowl

Choose a large capon up to 3 kg (7 lbs) in weight. Put into a saucepan and cover with water. Add to the liquid a carrot, 2 onions and some herbs, and simmer gently until tender (about 3 hours). Test by sticking a fork into the drum sticks. Remove from water and skin. Serve hot with boiled potatoes and ham.

Boiled Mutton

SERVES 8

If possible, use a home-killed animal and boil the same day. (Meat used really fresh is not tough, it gets tougher after a couple of days and then must be hung for a week or more before cooking.)

Choose a nice plump leg and boil it for 3 hours with bay leaves and rosemary. Serve with caper sauce.

Caper Sauce

2 tablespoons plain flour
600 ml (1 pint) milk
1 teaspoon salt
fresh black pepper
50 g (2 oz) butter
1 tablespoon capers

Mix the flour with a little of the milk and bring the rest of the milk to boil. When boiling add to the flour, stirring well. Add salt and pepper and butter, and finally, stir in the capers.

Batter Pudding

SERVES 4–6

300 ml (½ pint) milk
300 ml (½ pint) water
2 tablespoons plain flour
1 egg, beaten
salt and pepper
dripping

Mix all the ingredients (except dripping) together to form a thin batter and beat until it is really smooth. Place some dripping in a cooking pan, and when it is smoking, add the batter mixture. Bake for 20 minutes in a hot oven – 220ºC (425ºF) Gas 7.

Red Currant Jelly

1.5 kg (3 lbs) red currants
300 ml (½ pint) water
sugar (see below)

Strip the berries of all stalks. Put into a preserving pan with the water and boil gently until tender. Mash the fruit and strain overnight through a scalded jelly bag. To every 600 ml (1 pint) of juice, add 550 g (1¼ lbs) of warmed sugar. Stir over low heat until sugar has dissolved. Bring to the boil and boil rapidly until setting point has been reached. Test by putting a little in a saucer of cold water – it should coagulate. Pour into warm jars and seal.

Damson Tart

SERVES 6

900 g (2 lbs) firm damsons
3 tablespoons granulated sugar
600 ml (1 pint) water
1 teaspoon salt
225 g (8 oz) rough puff pastry (see page 141)

Wash the damsons and put them in a pie dish with the sugar, water and salt. Simmer them gently in a moderate oven until the damsons are soft, but not mushy. Let them cool, then cover them with rough puff pastry Return to a hot oven 200ºC (400ºF) Gas 6 until the pastry is nicely browned. Serve sprinkled with sugar.

Black Caps

(eighteenth-century recipe)

SERVES 6

Take out the cores of six large apples. Cut into halves. Place them on a thin patty-pan as closely as they can lie, with the flat side downwards. Squeeze half a lemon into one spoonful of orange flower water, and pour it over them. Shred some lemon peel finely, and throw it over them, and grate fine sugar over all. Set them in a quick oven, and half an hour will do them. Throw fine sugar all over the dish when you send to table.

Plain Custard

(eighteenth-century recipe)

SERVES 6

Set 600 ml (1 pint) of good cream over a slow fire, with a little cinnamon and 50 g (2 oz) of sugar. When it has boiled take it off the fire, beat the yolks of four eggs, and put to them a spoonful of orange flower water, to prevent the cream from cracking. Stir them in by degrees as your cream cools; put the pan over a very slow fire, stir it carefully one way till it be almost boiling, and then pour it into custard cups.

Blancmange

2 level tablespoons cornflour
2–3 level tablespoons castor sugar
600 ml (1 pint) milk

Mix the cornflour and sugar together with 2 tablespoons milk taken from the 600 ml (1 pint). Warm the rest of the milk and pour onto the mixture, stirring well. Return to the heat, bring to the boil and simmer for 1 minute, stirring all the time. Pour into a wetted mould and leave to set in a cool place.

Cochineal may be added to make a pink blancmange.

Bread and Cakes

Everything connected with the making of bread or yeast cooking should be warm.

Everything concerned with pastry must be as cool as possible. Never roll out pastry on a Formica top as this gives out heat. Instead use a wooden board or a stone slab.

Cornish Splits

Splits are the traditional soft bread rolls baked every day and sold in all the Cornish bakers' shops. I can only presume they are called 'splits' because the tradition is to cut or 'split' them in half and spread them with butter or cream and jam. Cornish clotted cream *(see page 179)* was always piled thickly on to them at tea-time. Splits are still much eaten by Cornishmen as well as by the millions of visitors who flock to the tea shops that advertise Cornish Cream Teas all over the West Country. A variation on the cream and jam theme was to spread the splits with cream and then pour golden syrup or treacle on top. This was known locally as 'thunder and lightning'.

Tea was an important meal to the Cornish. It was eaten when the menfolk returned from their work down the mines or in the fields and was likely to be the last meal of the day. Besides bread and splits, there may have been saffron cake *(see page 74)*, maybe part of a pasty left over from lunch or some cold bacon and pickles. It was not generally a cooked meal.

450 g (1 lb) flour
a good pinch of salt
50 g (2 oz) lard
25 g (1 oz) yeast
450 ml (¾ pint) warm milk
1 teaspoon sugar

Sift the flour and salt and rub the lard into it until it is all well absorbed. Put the yeast in a basin with 150 ml (¼ pint) of the warm milk and the sugar. Mix the remainder of the milk into the fat and flour, then finally stir in the yeast. Give the dough a good kneading and put in a bowl in a warm place to rise.

When risen turn out on a board dusted with flour. Cut into smallish rounds and put on a baking sheet. Leave to rise again, then bake in quick oven – 190ºC (375ºF) Gas 5 – until bottoms are brown – about 15 minutes.

Bread and Splits

THIS MAKES 2 LARGE LOAVES AND ABOUT 8 SPLITS

50 g (2 oz) lard
1–5 kg (3 lbs) strong flour
25 g (1 oz) salt
25 g (1 oz) fresh yeast
1 teaspoon sugar
900 ml (1½ pints) warm water (or half milk and water)

Rub the lard into the flour and add the salt. Put the yeast in a basin with the sugar and mix with 150 ml (¼ pint) of warm water. Make a well in the centre of the flour and pour in the yeast mixture. Sprinkle a little flour over the yeast and leave until yeast begins to break through flour. Add the rest of the warm water or milk and water and mix. Put on to a well-floured board and knead well. Return dough to bowl and leave to rise in a warm place, covered with a cloth. (It should double in size.)

When risen cut into three pieces and knead separately. Put two of these into well-greased bread tins and leave to rise again. Brush over with water and bake for 45 minutes at 220ºC (425ºF) Gas 7. To test, tap the bottom of the tin – they sound light if cooked.

Roll out the third piece about 2.5 cm (1 inch) thick and cut with a plain round cutter for 8 splits. Brush over with water and leave to rise. Bake in a slightly cooler oven for about 15 minutes.

Demelza used to make the bread at Nampara. There is a reference to it in *Demelza*, Book One, Chapter II and also in *The Black Moon*, Book One, Chapter XII:

While Ross was away Demelza had a caller . . . at the time she was baking bread. This she always did herself and would never leave to Jane Gimlett, who had a heavy hand. The bread was just beginning to plum when someone rat-tatted, on the front door. Jane came back and told her it was Miss Caroline Peneven . . .

Demelza took out as much of the dough as she could lift in her hands and put it on the board . . .

'Why do you knead each lump so long?' Caroline asked.

'Because if I don't the bread will have holes in it. We eat a lot of bread. There are five loaves here and a little over. Perhaps if I made you a small one with this smaller piece you would like to take it back with you?'

Demelza began to lift the round masses of kneaded dough on to a metal tray . . . . This part done, she stood back and rubbed her hands down her apron and then with the back of her wrist pushed the dank hair away from her eyes . . . . Presently they went back into the kitchen together and Demelza went under the arch of the stove, opened the iron door of the oven and raked out the white-hot remnants of the gorse. Then Caroline lifted the other end of the heavy tray and they slid it into the oven.

The oven referred to here is known as a cloam oven. This was generally a hole in the chimney wall, which was roofed over with a hard baked clay. The oven was heated by burning hedgerow trimmings such as gorse or blackthorn and it took about an hour to heat. When the oven was hot enough, the white-hot ashes were raked out, the food put in and the door shut, as indicated above.

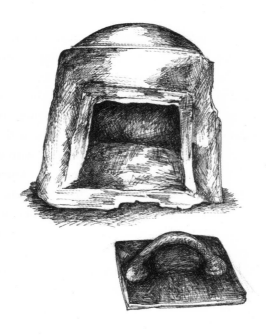

Lardy Bread

This was a tea-time treat that was a bit richer than ordinary bread.

225 g (8 oz) white bread dough (see page 113)
75 g (3 oz) lard
75 g (3 oz) granulated sugar
75 g (3 oz) dried fruit

Knead the dough well after its first rising and roll it out to a rectangular strip about 5 mm (¼ inch) thick. Cut the lard into small flakes and scatter a third of them over the surface and sprinkle over a third of the sugar and the fruit. Fold the dough over in thirds and roll out again. Scatter with another third of the lard flakes, sugar and fruit, roll up again and repeat the process once more. Roll up like a Swiss roll and put into a well-greased bread tin. Bake at 220°C (425°F) Gas 7 for about 35 minutes. Cool on a wire rack.

Yeast Cake

Another tea-time recipe that falls mid-way between a loaf of bread and a cake. They would be similar to the 'dough cakes' that Keren had brought with her on the night she eloped with Mark Daniel; see *Demelza*, Book One, Chapter VIII.

Yeast buns and yeast cake were also the traditional tea-time fare of the clay workers employed at the china clay works. This is a much younger industry than tin and copper mining; nevertheless nowadays a quarter of the world's supply of china clay comes from the West Country.

———◦◦◦———

100 g (4 oz) butter or lard
450 g (1 lb) flour
1 teaspoon salt
100 g (4 oz) currants
50 g (2 oz) sultanas
pinch nutmeg
100 g (4 oz) sugar
200 g (¾ oz) yeast
300 ml (½ pint) warm milk
½ teaspoon sugar

Rub the fat into the flour. Stir in the salt, fruit, nutmeg and sugar. Mix the yeast in a cup with a little warm milk and ½ teaspoon sugar. Make a well in the centre of mixture and add the yeast. Sprinkle lightly with flour. Leave until yeast breaks through the flour – about 3 minutes. Mix well to a dough, adding the remainder of the warm milk and leave in a warm place to rise.

Divide into two and put into two well-greased tins. Leave to rise again so they double in size. Bake in a moderate oven, about 180ºC (350ºF) Gas 4, for 1 hour.

Almond Cake

Ross found Verity in the parlour . . . Her face had become sallow under its tan and there were heavy shadows below her eyes.

'I had to see you, Ross. You understand better than the others. I had to see you about Andrew.'

'Sit down,' he said. 'I'll get you some ale and a slice of almond cake.'

Ross Poldark, Book One, Chapter XI

In the winter parlour Elizabeth had just excused herself and left again. Mr Odgers was finishing up the raspberry syllabub and Mrs Odgers the almond cake. With only the old lady's eyes on them, their manners had eased up.

Demelza, Book Three, Chapter II

───── ◦◦◦ ─────

175 g (6 oz) self-raising flour
pinch salt
25 g (1 oz) ground almonds
25 g (1 oz) ground rice
225 g (8 oz) butter
½ teaspoon almond essence
225 g (8 oz) fine sugar
4 eggs
milk to mix

Butter and line an 18 cm (7-inch) cake tin with greaseproof paper. Mix the flour, salt, ground almonds and ground rice together. Cream the butter with the almond essence and sugar until the mixture is pale and fluffy. Beat the eggs together and then beat them into the butter and sugar a little at a time. Fold the dry ingredients into the creamy mixture, adding a little milk if necessary to give a dropping consistency. Put into the tin, level the top and bake in the centre of the oven at 170°C (325°F) Gas 3 for 2–2¼ hours.

Plum Cake

ON THE OCCASION OF FRANCIS
AND ELIZABETH'S ENGAGEMENT.

Dinner was in progress at Trenwith House.

It would normally have been over by this time; when Charles Poldark and his family dined alone the meal seldom took more than two hours, but this was a special occasion . . .

'. . . Well I give you a toast. To the happy pair!'

'You've toasted that three times already,' objected Francis.

'No matter. Four is a luckier number.'

'But I cannot drink with you.'

'Hush boy! That's unimportant.'

Amid some laughter the toast was drunk. As the glasses clattered back upon the table lights were brought. Then the housekeeper, Mrs Tabb, arrived with the apple tarts, the plum cake and the jellies.

Ross Poldark, Book One, Chapter II

———— ◠◡◠ ————

225 g (8 oz) butter
225 g (8 oz) castor sugar
grated rind of lemon
4 eggs
2 teaspoons glycerine

275 g (10 oz) plain flour
¼ teaspoon salt
100 g (4 oz) mixed peel
450 g (1 lb) cherries, raisins and currants
50 g (2 oz) chopped blanched almonds
3 tablespoons brandy

Line a 20 cm (8-inch) cake tin with buttered grease-proof paper. Cream the butter with the sugar and grated lemon rind. Beat in the well-beaten eggs a little at a time and then add the glycerine. Sift the flour and salt together and fold a third into the cake mixture. Add the mixed fruit and almonds and then fold in the remainder of the flour and salt. Put into cake tin and bake in warm oven 170ºC (325ºF) Gas 3 for half an hour. Reduce heat to 150ºC (300ºF) Gas 2 and cook for a further 2½ hours.

When the cake is quite cold, turn it over and make some holes in the bottom with a skewer. Pour the brandy into these, then wrap the cake in paper and store for at least 3 weeks.

'Jeremy's Christening'

It was just a small party at Nampara House: Francis and Elizabeth and Andrew Blarney and Verity – and Dwight Enys, who was now almost one of the family. Not a christening party for Jeremy, because it was natural to shrink from repeating anything which had happened in Julia's life; this marked the opening of Wheal Grace – the first men engaged, the first sods broken. Demelza, handicapped by weakness and a delicate baby, had left ail the catering to the Gimletts, and they'd done well enough. Boiled cod with oyster sauce, a piece of boiled beef, roast neck of pork, two small turkeys with ham, fried rabbits, a plum pudding, tartlets and pies – with apples and olives and almonds and raisins for dessert. Demelza looked round and thought: This is much more than we can afford, but of course it's quite right not to skimp for such an occasion.

Jeremy Poldark, Book Two, Chapter XIV

NOTE: See page 147 for boiled cod and oyster sauce.

Boiled Beef

SERVES 12

Put a piece of brisket about 2.75 kg (6 lbs) in weight into a brine solution and leave for one week.

Take out and wash well. Put into a large pan of cold water, add 1 onion, 2 carrots and some parsley. Bring to the boil and then simmer gently for 3 hours. Serve with extra carrots and dumplings.

Turkey with Ham

SERVES 8

Choose a hen turkey, rather small, if possible weighing no more than 3.5 kg (8 lbs). Stuff with parsley and breadcrumbs mixed together with an egg and some salt. Roast in a hot oven – 220ºC (425ºF) Gas 7 – having well buttered the breast and legs. Cook for 2 hours, basting every 30 minutes.

Serve this with a piece of boiled ham, well spiced with cloves *(see page 99)*.

Fried Rabbit

1 RABBIT SERVES 3 PEOPLE

Choose young rabbits. Skin them and wash well in salt water. Cut each rabbit into seven joints: i.e. 4 legs and 3 thick pieces of back bone. Dry well on absorbent paper and dip in seasoned flour. Fry in butter until tender and brown.

Plum Pudding

This is an alternative recipe
to the one on page 47.

350 g (12 oz) sultanas
350 g (12 oz) currants
225 g (8 oz) stoned raisins
50 g (2 oz) sweet almonds, chopped and skinned
225 g (8 oz) mixed candied peel, chopped
450 g (1 lb) soft brown sugar
225 g (8 oz) fine breadcrumbs
350 g (12 oz) shredded beef suet
1 level teaspoon mixed spice
1 level teaspoon salt
7 eggs
1 wine glass brandy
75 ml (½ gill) stout
juice of 1 lemon
300 ml (½ pint) milk
1 level teaspoon grated nutmeg

Grease three 500 ml (1 pint) pudding basins. Pick over and wash the fruit. Mix all the dry ingredients together in a large bowl. Beat the eggs well and mix with the brandy, stout and lemon juice. Stir this into the dry ingredients, adding enough milk to make the mixture into a moist consistency.

Put the mixture into the prepared pudding basins. Cover with cloths and boil steadily for 7 hours. Take the puddings out, and when cold cover them with clean dry cloths. Store in a cool place till needed. When required boil again for 2 hours before serving.

Sweet Egg Pie

(eighteenth-century recipe)

SERVES 6

Use a fairly deep pie dish and line it with good pastry. Cover it with six hard-boiled eggs sliced fine and dot 100 g (4 oz) butter between them. Cover the eggs with 225 g (8 oz) cleaned currants. Beat 4 eggs; mix with 300 ml (½ pint) white wine, a little nutmeg and sweeten with fine sugar. Pour this into the dish and cover with pastry. Bake at 200ºC (400ºF) Gas 6 until pastry is brown.

Pasties

The now famous pasty came into existence towards the end of the eighteenth century. According to the *St James' Chronicle* they were for the 'lowest sort of people' and comprised no more than 'vegetables wrapped up in a black barley crust'. The pie is older fare than the pasty in Cornwall, but the pasty was found to be more convenient for the miners and farm labourers to take to work and eat at mid-day. In early times they rarely contained meat (indeed many families had meat no more than once or twice in three months) and were made primarily of turnip and potato. As time went on, they became more nourishing and sophisticated and endless variations of filling were devised. I particularly remember rabbit pasties, in which the ribs of the rabbit were used to hold out the pastry! Pasties can have sweet fillings too – apple and blackberry or jam – and they would then be served with sugar and cream.

Pasties do not feature greatly in Poldark fare; they were served at the Warleggans' House with cakes and jellies, syllabubs and fruits, punch and wines and tea and coffee after the Lord Lieutenant's Ball; see *Demelza*, Book Two, Chapter XI.

Family pasties always had the person's initial on the pasty at the corner. One reason for this was that some liked a lot of onion, others none; some liked pepper and so on. One person I knew liked a 'poor pasty'. That meant she did not want too much meat, but some really big pieces of fat. The corner with the initial was usually kept for tea-time.

In early summer we had pasties made entirely of new potatoes sliced finely, with salt and pepper, and when they were cooked we made a hole in the top and put a big dollop of cream in. Nobody thought of carbohydrates or cholesterol; the Cornish people were hard-working on the farms and in the mines and did not have to worry about such things.

At the local council school, which was in a wooded valley two miles from the village, the children would race out of the school yard at dinner-time and run up a small lane, each one clutching his or her pasty. Each one had a favourite branch in the scrub oaks which grew on the banks of the lane, the best place of course being the highest where one had the best view. There they would sit like a flock of starlings eating their pasties until the school bell clanged out to go back to the classrooms.

Meat and Potato Pasty

The ingredients for a meat pasty must be raw – you cannot use any cooked left-overs from a joint. The best type of meat is sirloin skirt because it has fat running through it and this makes it tender.

———— ◆ ————

THIS QUANTITY OF PASTRY
MAKES 3–4 PASTIES
225 g (8 oz) rough puff pastry (see page 141)

TO EACH PASTY
100 g (4 oz) raw meat
3 medium-sized potatoes
1 small onion
milk
salt and pepper

Roll out pastry about 5 mm (¼ inch) thick and use a plate to cut out a circle of about 15 cm (6 inches) diameter. Chop the meat finely, peel and thinly slice the potato and onion. Put the potato slices in the middle of the pastry; cover with the meat and sliced onion. Season well. Moisten the edge of the pastry with a little water and bring edges up across the filling. Pinch together firmly.

To make the crinkle, hold the edges of pastry firmly

with the first finger and thumb of the left hand, then twist the edges over each other with the right hand until they are firmly joined. You should have an oblong object, like a closed purse.

Brush over with milk and put on to a greased flat tin. Bake at 230°C (450°F) Gas 8 for the first 20 minutes then lower temperature to 190°C (375°F) Gas 5 and bake for a further half an hour.

Leek Pasty

This pasty was made as a supper dish for the whole family so it was very large. It was served in thick slices, traditionally on Thursday nights after the market, but it was kept warm all day on the rack of the stove.

———— ◡ ————

SERVES 6
225 g (8 oz) rough puff pastry (see page 141)
6 leeks
3 slices belly pork or bacon
2 eggs
salt and pepper

Roll out the pastry on a well-floured board, to a thickness of about 1 cm (½ inch) and cut a circle with a large dinner plate about 20 cm (8 inches) in diameter. Trim and wash the leeks well, then cut them into rings. Put into a colander and pour 1.2 litres (a quart) of boiling water on top of them. (This blanches them, but keeps the green part a good colour.) Drain and dry thoroughly in a cloth. Put the leeks onto the pastry and dot with small pieces of pork or bacon. Seal up both ends leaving a hole in the middle. Into this put the two eggs, gently breaking the yolks so that they run down among the leeks and bacon. Seal firmly.

Bake for 20 minutes at 230ºC (450ºF) Gas 8 at the top of the oven. Lower heat to 190ºC (375ºF) Gas 5 and put pasty on lower rung. Cook for another 40 minutes, then remove from oven and keep warm until needed. Serve by cutting in thick slices.

NOTE: As this is such a large pasty it is easier if you put your rolling pin under the top side of the pastry to prop it up.

Turnip and Potato Pasty

Turnips in the West Country are *always* the yellow type, usually referred to in other parts of the country as swedes. When I was a child they were 1d each.

Use the same method of preparation as for the Meat and Potato Pasty, covering the potato with thinly sliced turnip and a little onion. Season well and cook as for the Meat and Potato Pasty.

Minced Beef Pasty

These were made to be eaten cold, and were always small – no more than about 10 cm (4 inches) long. This quantity makes about 8 pasties.

225 g (8 oz) rough puff pastry (see below)
350 g (12 oz) beef skirt
1 large onion
salt and pepper

Roll out pastry and cut into 10 cm (4 inch) diameter circles. Mince beef finely and pile it in the middle of the pastry. Add a little chopped onion and salt and pepper. Bake for half an hour at 190ºC (375ºF) Gas 5.

Parsley Pasty

These were also small, although they were eaten hot.

———— ❧ ————

MAKES ABOUT 8 PASTIES

225 g (8 oz) rough puff pastry (see below)
large bunch of parsley
2 eggs
salt and pepper

Wash and chop a large bunch of parsley very finely. Place on small pastry circles. Season well. Crinkle ends of pastry together and leave a small hole in the middle. Beat 2 eggs well in a cup, add seasoning, then pour a little of the beaten egg into each pasty. Seal pastry and bake pasties for 20 minutes at 190ºC (375ºF) Gas 5.

Rough Puff Pastry

Make this quantity when a recipe states 225 g (8 oz) rough puff pastry.

———— ❧ ————

225 g (8 oz) self-raising flour
1 teaspoon salt
75 g (3 oz) hard margarine
75 g (3 oz) lard
7 tablespoons cold water

Sift the flour into a bowl with the salt. Cut the fat into the flour (don't make the pieces too small). Make sure each piece of fat is coated with flour. Add the water and mix together with a palette knife to a firm, non-sticky dough.

Flour a pastry board and rolling pin and roll out the pastry into an oblong piece. Fold into three, and give the pastry a half turn, so that the folded edges are on the right and left. Repeat the rolling and turning until the pastry has been rolled five times. If possible leave for 15 minutes in a cool place between the rollings and before using.

'Ralph-Allen Daniell's Dinner Party'

They ate and they drank and they ate. Boiled cod with fried soles and oyster sauce; roast beef and orange pudding; wild duck with asparagus and mushroom; fricandeau of veal with sage stuffing and high sauce. After this there were syllabubs, jellies, apricot tarts, lemon puddings and sweet pies. And madeira and claret and Rhine wine and port and brandy.

The Black Moon, Book One, Chapter VIII

NOTE: see page 180 for recipe for Syllabub.

Boiled Cod

SERVES 6
900 g (2 lbs) cod
2 small shallots
small bunch parsley
salt and pepper

Wash the fish well and put it in a saucepan. Cover with cold water and add the shallots, parsley and salt and pepper. Simmer gently until fish is cooked – about 35 minutes. Drain, and serve with oyster sauce.

Oyster Sauce

Scald 600 ml (1 pint) of large oysters and strain them through a sieve. Wash them well in cold water and take off die beards. Put them into a stew pan and cover with clear cold water. Add a spoonful of anchovy sauce, half a lemon and 2 blades of mace. Bring to the boil and thicken with a lump of butter rolled in flour. Add 100 g (4 oz) butter and boil gently until the butter is melted. Take out the mace and add the juice of half a lemon. Bring gently back to the boil and pour over the cod.

Roast Beef

Choose either a piece of standing rib or wing rib. Sprinkle with salt and spread some good beef dripping over the joint. Roast in a hot oven 220°C (425°F) Gas 7, allowing 20 minutes to the 450 g (1 lb) and basting regularly. Serve with horseradish sauce.

Orange Pudding

to go with Roast Beef

SERVES 6–8
175 g (6 oz) suet pastry (see below)
4 oranges
300 ml (½ pint) milk
75 g (3 oz) sugar
100 g (4 oz) cake crumbs
2 eggs
pinch nutmeg

Line a 1.6 litre (2 pint) pie dish with suet pastry. Stew the rind of one orange in the milk; then remove from the heat. Add the sugar, cake crumbs, well-beaten eggs and nutmeg to the milk. Then add the juice of the oranges. Pour this mixture into the pastry and bake at 190°C (375°F) Gas 5 until the pastry is cooked and the mixture set.

Suet Pastry

50 g (4 oz) beef suet
100 g (8 oz) plain flour
1 teaspoon salt
7 tablespoons water

Chop the suet finely with a little flour. Sift the remaining flour and salt and add the suet. Mix to a firm dough with cold water. Roll out and use as required.

Wild Duck

This has a very strong flavour, so it is necessary to keep the accessories only lightly seasoned.

Stuff the duck with sage and onions and put into a roasting pan with a little water. Do not put any fat on the bird as sufficient will come out during cooking. Baste frequently. Cook for 1¼ hours in a fairly hot oven – 200°C (400°F) Gas 6.

Asparagus and Mushrooms

to go with Wild Duck

Asparagus was once cultivated in large quantities at Kynance Cove. English asparagus is fat but greener than the French.

———— ◆ ————

Trim the large white ends of the asparagus. Scrape the stalks with a sharp knife, taking care not to damage the tips. Wash well in cold water. Tie them in small bundles with the heads all in one direction. Stand up in a pan of salted water (heads at the top out of the water). By the time the stem is cooked the tips should be tender. Drain and serve with melted butter and lemon juice.

Mushrooms can be either fried in butter or cooked in milk in the oven. Wash them well and trim the stalks. Peel off the skin if necessary.

To cook in the oven, put the mushrooms in a deep pan and cover with milk; add salt and pepper and simmer gently until tender.

To fry, cook gently in melted bacon fat until tender.

Fricandeau of Veal

SERVES 6

900 g (2 lbs) piece of best veal
2 onions
2 carrots
1 turnip
2 heads celery
25 g (1 oz) bacon
25 g (1 oz) butter or lard
parsley
rosemary
sage and thyme
600 ml (1 pint) beef stock
salt and pepper
700 g (1½ lbs) sorrel (optional)

Roughly chop all the vegetables and the bacon. Melt the fat and fry the vegetables and bacon together until slightly brown. Lay the veal on top and fry gently. Put all the ingredients except the sorrel into a deep earthenware dish, pouring the stock on top. Simmer gently for 1 hour. Cook the sorrel in salted water until tender and serve with the meat.

High Sauce to go with Veal

2 carrots
2 onions
1 parsnip
1 potato
100 g (4 oz) ham
2 cloves garlic, crushed
25 g (1 oz) butter
25 g (1 oz) flour
300 ml (½ pint) stock
1 tablespoon grated horseradish
6 peppercorns
1 tablespoon chopped chervil
½ teaspoon dried herbs
1 Seville orange
1 lemon
1 tumbler red wine
pinch of sugar
freshly ground pepper

Slice the carrots, onions, parsnip and potato. Chop the ham. Melt the butter and fry the ham, then add the sliced vegetables and crushed garlic and cook until nicely browned. Add the flour and cook, stirring until it browns. Add the stock, horseradish, peppercorns, chervil and dried herbs and simmer for 30 minutes. Then strain.

To the strained liquor, add the rind of half the Seville

orange cut into thin strips. Squeeze the juice from the orange and the lemon and add this with the red wine, sugar and pepper. Reheat and serve hot.

Apricot Tart

SERVES 6
24 fresh apricots
sugar
cinnamon
225 g (8 oz) short crust pastry (see below)

Put the apricots in a deep pie dish and cover with water and sugar. Stew gently. When the apricots are soft remove from heat, cut in half and remove stones. Line a shallow dish with stewed apricots. Sprinkle with a little sugar and add some of the liquid in which the fruit was stewed. Sprinkle with a little cinnamon. Cover with short crust pastry and bake in hot oven – 200ºC (400ºF) Gas 6 – for about 30 minutes. Brush the top of the pie lightly with water and dredge well with castor sugar. Return to oven quickly and allow to brown.

Short Crust Pastry

Make this quantity when a recipe states 225 g (8 oz) short crust pastry.

225 g (8 oz) plain flour
½ teaspoon salt
100 g (4 oz) fat [50 g (2 oz) butter; 50 g (2 oz) lard]
1 egg yolk, beaten
ice-cold water

Sift the flour and salt. Rub the fat into the flour with finger tips until the mixture is like fine breadcrumbs. Add the egg yolk and mix well. If the mixture is too stiff add a tablespoonful of the cold water. Roll out and use as required.

NOTE: There is *no* glazing on fruit tarts. They are usually dusted with castor sugar or icing sugar.

Lemon Pudding

SERVES 6–8

8 eggs
100 g (4 oz) butter
225 g (8 oz) fine sugar
8 lemons
100 g (4 oz) flour
900 ml (1½ pints) milk

Separate the yolks from the whites of the eggs. Cream the butter and sugar; then add the grated rind and juice of the lemons. Beat in the flour and milk, and lastly the egg yolks. Beat egg whites until stiff and fold into mixture. Put into a well-greased pie dish and stand in a baking dish of water. Bake in a cool oven – 150ºC (300ºF) Gas 2 – until set – about 45 minutes. Serve hot with cream.

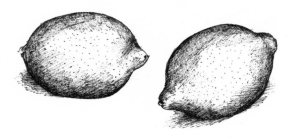

Sauces, Chutneys
and Preserves

Sauces were little used by the poor in their everyday meals, but like everything else were always in great demand at the banqueting tables of the big houses. I personally think they tended to be, and still are, overused.

Basic White Sauce

1 tablespoon plain flour
600 ml (1 pint) milk
50 g (2 oz) butter
salt and freshly ground black pepper

Mix the flour to a paste with a little water. Put the milk on to boil. When boiling, add the flour paste, stirring rapidly. Add the butter and seasoning.

NOTE: To make Parsley Sauce, use the above method, adding a level tablespoon of finely chopped parsley.

Egg Sauce

Serve this with boiled cod.

2 hard-boiled eggs
225 g (8 oz) butter
salt

Chop the hard-boiled eggs roughly. Melt the butter and stir into the chopped egg. Season with salt.

Bread Sauce

1 large onion
4 cloves
300 ml (1½ pints) fresh milk
50 g (2 oz) dry white breadcrumbs
25 g (1 oz) butter
salt and pepper

Stick the onion with the cloves and put in a small pan with the milk. Add the breadcrumbs and some salt and pepper. Let the mixture simmer very gently for 30 minutes, giving it an occasional stir. Remove onion and add the butter. Serve at once.

Cranberry Sauce

225 g (8 oz) cranberries
300 ml (½ pint) water
sugar to taste

Put the cranberries in a pan with 150 ml (¼ pint) water and stew until soft. Gradually add the remainder of the water. Put the mixture through a fine sieve and add sugar to taste. Reheat before serving.

For economy you can use half sour cooking apples in place of half the cranberries.

Sorrel Sauce

Sorrel is known locally in Cornwall as Sour Sabs

Take a handful of sorrel and beat it in a mortar with two sweet apples pared and quartered. Add a little vinegar and sugar. This is a green sauce and often used with white fish.

Pickled Beetroot

Boil beetroot until tender and cut into shapes as you please. Pour over it a hot pickle of white wine vinegar and a little ginger and pepper and sliced horseradish. Store in jars and cover tightly with paper.

Aunt Agatha's Chutney

Any left-over meats, stale bread or tired cheese can be made interesting by the addition of a pickled onion or a spoonful of this chutney.

---

450 g (1 lb) Piccalilli
450 g (1 lb) gooseberry jam
handful of sultanas
cayenne pepper

Chop the Piccalilli roughly and put with the gooseberry jam and the sultanas into a saucepan. Cook until the Piccalilli is soft. Add a pinch of cayenne pepper and pour into warm jars.

For Ross the early part of the winter was endless. For days on end the driving mists filled the valley until the walls of Nampara House ran with damp and the stream was in yellow spate . . .

Only Verity came often. She was his contact with the rest of the family, bringing him gossip and companionship . . .

One day in mid-March she came . . . and brought him some jars of her own preserves . . .

Ross Poldark, Book One, Chapter V

In fact, there has never been a great tradition among Cornish housewives for making preserves, apart from jam to eat with the splits and cream. Mostly produce was eaten as it was picked, rather than preserved for later consumption.

Preserved Quince

(eighteenth-century recipe)

Quinces may be preserved whole or in quarters. Peel them very thin and put them into a saucepan. Cover with water and lay the parings on top to keep the quinces submerged. Cover the pan with a tight-fitting lid and put over a slow heat until the quinces are soft and a fine pink colour. Then let them stand until cold.

Make a thickish syrup of sugar and water. Let it boil, then skim it well. Add the quinces and boil for 10 minutes. Let them stand for 3 hours. Boil again until the syrup looks thick and the quinces clear. Put into deep, warm jars and cover tightly.

Red Gooseberry Preserve

(eighteenth-century recipe)

Take 450 g (1 lb) lump sugar. Put it into a preserving pan with as much water as will dissolve it. Boil and take off scum as it rises. Add 1.2 l (1 quart) of red gooseberries and let them boil a little but not sufficient to break them. Let them stand until the next day. Boil again until they look clear and the syrup is thick. Let them cool. Then bottle in glass jars and cover with brandy paper.* Cover with thin muslin and tie down.

---

* Brandy paper is made by cutting white paper into circles a little larger than the tops of the jars. Let the paper steep in brandy until well soaked through.

Preserved Figs

Cornwall is a good place for green figs. They rarely ripen but are excellent for preserving. This is another old recipe.

50–100 figs (or as many as you wish)
2 tablespoons lime juice
1 teaspoon alum
1 tablespoon salt
lemon juice
sugar (see below)
water (see below)

Peel each fig very thinly and cut a slit across the top. Put the lime into a bowl of water and add the figs. Put a weight on top to stop the figs from floating to the surface and leave for 12 hours. Take out the figs and wash them thoroughly.

Put 3.5 l (3 quarts) of cold water into a saucepan with the figs. Add the alum and salt and lemon juice. Boil until figs are soft. Drain the figs and weigh them. Take the same weight of sugar plus an extra 450 g (1 lb). Take one cup of water to one cup of sugar and put into a saucepan until you have used all the sugar. Boil this until the syrup is clear. Then add the figs and boil again until they are clear.

'Demelza's Dinner
Party for the Bassets'

So the dinner came off on a fine Tuesday in mid-February. Demelza had given great thought to the menu, for she knew, whatever Ross might think, that she would have to oversee the meal until the last second. She did pease soup, which could be got ready beforehand, then a boiled tongue, similarly easy, followed by a fat little turkey hen roasted, with chopped bacon, then her special raspberry jam puffs, and ended with a syllabub and mince pies.

The Four Swans, Book Two, Chapter V

NOTE: see page 180 for a recipe for syllabub and page 49 for a recipe for mince pies.

Pea Soup

SERVES 6

450 g (1 lb) dried peas
900 g (2 lbs) slightly salted green bacon
2 leeks
bunch each of parsley and thyme, chopped
2 small potatoes

Put the peas to soak overnight. Next morning, cook them in 1.75 l (3 pints) of water. Add the bacon, chopped leeks, herbs and peeled and sliced potatoes. Simmer until bacon is tender. Take out bacon and pour soup into tureen.

NOTE: The bacon can be served separately.

Boiled Tongue

To boil a salted tongue, first steep it in cold water overnight. Then boil it gently for 3 hours. Test to see if it is cooked by pinching the tip of the tongue; this is the toughest part. If it is still hard, cook for a little longer. When cooked, skin the tongue while it is still hot and remove the small bones at the base.

If it is to be eaten hot, flick it over with cloves, then rub it over with the yolk of an egg. Strew some crumbled bread over it, baste with melted butter and set it before the fire or in the oven till the breadcrumbs are light brown. Serve it with a good brown gravy or red wine sauce and lay slices of red currant jelly round it.

If the tongue is wanted cold, after skinning and removing the bones, put into a round deep cake tin and cover with greaseproof paper. Put a plate on top with a heavy weight on it to keep the tongue firmly pressed down. Leave in a cool place.

NOTE: Demelza would have bought a tongue from a local farmer and then put it to steep in an earthenware dish with salt and saltpetre for at least a week. Nowadays, tongues are usually salted by the butcher. Saltpetre is still used as it keeps the meat a good colour.

Demelza's Hen Turkey

Select a turkey weighing 4.5–5.5 kg (10–12 lbs). Stuff crop with veal stuffing and put chestnut stuffing in body (see below). Cover breast with a few slices of bacon and cook at 220°C (425°F) Gas 7 for 30 minutes. Reduce heat to 190°C (375°F) Gas 5 and continue cooking, basting frequently. Allow 15 minutes per 450 g (1 lb) for turkey under 6 kg (14 lbs) weight. Remove bacon to brown breast about 20 minutes before the end of the cooking time. Serve with bread sauce or cranberry sauce *(see pages p162, 163).*

Chestnut Stuffing

900 g (2 lbs) chestnuts
300 ml (½ pint) chicken stock
50 g (2 oz) butter
salt and pepper

Slit the chestnuts and boil them for 20 minutes. Then remove the outer shells and inner skin. Stew again in sufficient stock to cover them. When they are tender, rub them through a fine wire sieve. Add the butter and seasoning and mix to a soft 'doughy' texture.

Veal Stuffing

225 g (8 oz) veal
100 g (4 oz) belly pork
1 onion
1 large mushroom
100 g (4 oz) fine breadcrumbs
1 teaspoon chopped parsley
1 egg, beaten
salt and pepper

Chop and mince the veal and pork. Chop the onion and mushroom finely. Mix all these together well with the breadcrumbs and chopped parsley. Season to taste and bind with the beaten egg.

If the mixture is too dry, add a little cold milk.

Raspberry Puffs

Make some good puff pastry *(see page 141)*. Roll out to about 1 cm (½ inch) thick and cut into circles with a round pastry cutter. Put on to slightly damp baking sheets (the moisture helps the pastry to rise). Brush lightly with milk, and bake at 220°C (425°F) Gas 7 for 15 minutes by which time the puffs should have risen well.

Lift off the trays carefully and cool on a wire rack. When cold, slice through the middle of each circle and spread one side with either fresh raspberries and cream or raspberry jam and cream. Put the other slice on top and dust with icing sugar.

Cornish Cream

Cornish clotted cream, or clouted cream, as it was originally called, is in fact scalded cream. Cornish housewives used to (and in many instances still do) make cream daily. You can make it in any quantity – small, or large – from the recipe below, just 600–1000 ml (1 pint or 2) of milk can be used.

———— ∾ ————

Use only very fresh milk. Pour it into a large bowl or basin, and stand in a cool place for 12 hours in summer and 24 hours in winter to allow the cream to rise.

Put the bowl into a large saucepan containing water, and let the water slowly heat until the cream begins to show a raised ring around the edge. *On no account* let the milk boil. Place in a cool dairy or larder and leave for 12 hours. Great care must be taken when moving the pans so that the cream is not broken. Skim the cream off in layers into a glass dish, choosing a nice crusty piece for the top.

Syllabub

This is among the most frequently mentioned of all sweets and puddings in the Poldark books. In fact, Syllabub was not peculiarly Cornish, but was widely popular in the eighteenth century, doubtless because it uses easily acquired ingredients.

SERVES 6–8
2 lemons
4 teaspoons sherry
4 teaspoons brandy
175 g (6 oz) castor sugar
600 ml (1 pint) double cream
pinch of ground cinnamon

Carefully grate the rind of the lemons. Squeeze the juice and leave to stand together for several hours. Add the sherry and brandy to the lemon juice, then add the sugar, stirring until dissolved. Whip the cream, taking care not to let it curdle. Carefully blend the lemon mixture into the cream, adding a little at a time until a soft curd is produced.

Serve in individual glasses, sprinkled with a pinch of cinnamon.

Puddings

Friar's Omelet

This is an eighteenth-century recipe which has more in common with Apple Charlotte than a conventional omelette.

———— ∾ ————

SERVES 6

675 g (1½ lbs) apples
75 g (3 oz) sugar
150 ml (1 gill) of water
40 g (1½ oz) butter
300 ml (½ pint) white breadcrumbs
a few brown breadcrumbs
extra sugar

Peel and core the apples. Slice them and stew with the sugar and water until soft. Add butter.

Butter a pie dish and sprinkle in some of the white breadcrumbs. Fill with alternate layers of apples and the remaining white breadcrumbs. Sprinkle the top with brown crumbs and bake in a hot oven – 200ºC (400ºF) Gas 6 for 10 minutes.

Turn out on to a hot dish, sprinkle with castor sugar and serve hot.

Damson Cheese

Another eighteenth-century recipe for when damsons are plentiful.

———⟡———

Bake 1.5 kg (3 lbs) damsons until they split, then put them with 450 g (1 lb) sugar in a pan and boil until they turn into a stiff jam, taking out the stones as they rise. Crack the stones, peel the kernels and put them back into the pan. Keep boiling until the puree becomes very stiff. Put the cheese into round cups or deep plates, and keep near the fire for a week to dry. Removed from the cups and put in oiled paper, it makes a pretty plate for supper.

Wine or Sweet Biscuits

We used to eat these with a glass of sherry on special occasions.

———— ❧ ————

450 g (1 lb) flour
350 g (12 oz) butter
100 g (4 oz) castor sugar
¾ teaspoon ammonia

Rub the butter into the flour and stir in the sugar. Dissolve the ammonia in ½ teaspoon of warm water and mix together well. Stir into the biscuit mixture and mix to a dough. Roll out to about 1 cm (½ inch) thick and cut out biscuits. Bake in a hot oven – 220°C (450°F) Gas 7 – until brown.

Remove from the baking sheet with a sharp knife.

Jelly

Jelly was popular Poldark fare, served as pudding on many occasions.

———— ❧ ————

SERVES 6

Take some large veal bones. Chop them so they fit into a large saucepan; cover with water and simmer for 3 hours. Strain off liquid into a bowl. Beat 4 egg whites together well and add the crushed shells to them. Put into a jelly cloth over a bowl and pour the liquid over. This should clear the liquid. If it does not, repeat until the liquid does run clear.

Rinse a litre (2 pint) jelly mould with clean cold water. Put the jelly liquid into a saucepan with 2 tablespoons of fine sugar, 2 drops of cochineal and a few drops of vanilla essence. Heat until the sugar is dissolved, then pour into the mould and put in a cool place to set.

Aunt Emma's Figgy 'Obbin

'Figgy' is a Cornish term for raisins. Aunt Emma was a great-great-aunt of mine, and this is her recipe – a sort of Cornish 'Spotted Dick'.

———— ❧ ————

SERVES 6

225 g (8 oz) plain flour
1 teaspoon baking powder
50 g (2 oz) butter
100 g (4 oz) suet
75 g (3 oz) sugar
100 g (4 oz) raisins
pinch of salt
1 egg
a little milk

Mix the flour with the baking powder and rub in the butter. Chop the suet finely and add to the butter and flour with all the remaining dry ingredients. Mix to a firm dough with beaten egg and a little milk. Lightly flour a pastry board and roll out the mixture into an oblong. Roll up and seal the ends.

Put into a well-greased tin and bake for half an hour at 180°C (350°F) Gas 4 until nicely browned.

Apple Fritters

SERVES 6

FOR THE BATTER
1 egg
100 g (4 oz) plain flour
150 ml (1 gill) milk
pinch of salt
450 g (1 lb) cooking apples
juice of 1 lemon
little castor sugar

Make the batter; beat the egg and add to flour with milk and salt. Beat until smooth.

To make the fritters: peel the apples and core them. Cut into rings about 5 mm (¼ inch) thick and lay on a plate. Sprinkle with lemon juice and sugar. Let them stand for a few minutes, then dip in batter and fry in deep fat until nicely brown.

Apple Frazes

Mrs Richard Polwhele's cook, in following the above recipe, was instructed to steep the apples in brandy for at least six hours, then use the brandy in the batter mixture, adding rosewater, cinnamon, white wine and stout.

Chervil or Spinach Tart

(eighteenth-century recipe)

SERVES 6
4.5 l (1 gallon) spinach or chervil
225 g (8 oz) melted butter
3 lemons
450 g (1 lb) sugar
225 g (8 oz) puff pastry (see page 141)
cream or custard
fine sugar

Wash and shred the spinach very finely. Pour melted butter on to it. Add the pulp of the lemons, free of skin or seeds, with the grated rind of two of the lemons and the sugar. Put the mixture into either patty-pans or a dish and cover with the pastry. When the pastry is nicely brown take off the pastry lid and put cream or custard over the spinach filling. Shake some fine sugar on top and replace lid. Serve cold.

Poldark Trifle

This is a modern recipe, but I feel justified in giving it its name as I made it in large quantity for a party we gave at my husband's London club for members of the cast of the original television series. There were about seventy guests, and, although the club was providing the rest of the food, I rashly volunteered to make the trifle.

For this I used 6 lbs of Cornish cream (brought up specially that day by my daughter), 8 pints of ordinary double cream, and 12 pints of custard. The other amounts were 12 packets of sponge cakes, 6 lbs of blackcurrant jam, 48 bananas, 6 tins of apricots and 3 bottles of rum. And a large quantity of angelica, cherries and almonds.

Here the recipe is given with the ingredients in more normal quantities.

SERVES 8–10
8 sponge cakes
blackcurrant jam
5 bananas
1 tin apricots
¼ bottle rum
900 ml (1½ pints) sweet custard
1.2 l (2 pints) cream
angelica, cherries and blanched almonds

Cut the sponge cakes in half and spread generously with blackcurrant jam. Put these into a cut-glass dish. Slice the bananas and drain the apricots, reserving the juice. Cover the sponge cakes with the fruit and add the rum and the apricot juice. Cover with hot custard.

Leave until cold. Pour 600 ml (1 pint) of the cream over the custard. Lightly whip the other pint and spread on top. Decorate with angelica, cherries and almonds.

Lemon Meringue Pie

SERVES 6–8

FOR PASTRY
100 g (4 oz) plain flour
50 g (2 oz) hard margarine
1 egg yolk
4 teaspoons water

FOR FILLING
rind and juice of 1 lemon
4 level tablespoons cornflour
100 g (4 oz) castor sugar
300 ml (½ pint) water
25 g (1 oz) margarine
2 egg yolks

FOR MERINGUE
3 egg whites
150 g (5 oz) caster sugar

Make the pastry as for short crust *(see page 155)*, adding the egg yolk with the water. Roll out and line a shallow ovenproof dish with pastry.

Grate the lemon rind and squeeze the juice. Put into a saucepan. Add the cornflour, sugar and water. Stir over low heat until blended and thickened. Beat in the egg yolks and the margarine. Fill the pastry with the lemon mixture and lightly bake for 10 minutes at 150°C (300°F) Gas 2.

Beat the egg whites for the meringue with 50 g (2 oz) sugar until stiff. Fold in the remaining sugar and spoon the meringue on top of the lemon filling. Sprinkle a little sugar on top of the meringue and bake at 180°C (350°F) Gas 4 until the meringue is set and lightly browned.

Wines and Drinks

On our farms, the women, as well as the men, have at particular seasons their morning drams before the commencement of the work. And the brandy-glass circulates briskly among the farmers, before any occasional dinner, immediately after the dinner, and a third time before the breaking up of the company: this latter is called the stirrup-glass, and is generally given by the master of the house to his departing guests when mounted at his door. Among the miners, and others, spiritous liquors are equally in repute.

Polwhele on Drinking (1803)

Punch

Such drinks as these have long been popular in Cornwall and probably originated during the heyday of the smuggling 'industry'. The kiddleys, or beer houses, situated along the coast would often sell contraband rum, brandy and gin very cheaply.

———————◆———————

MAKES 8 GLASSFULS
1 large lemon
50–75 g (2–3 oz) loaf sugar
pinch ground cinnamon
pinch grated nutmeg
3 cloves
300 ml (½ pint) brandy
300 ml (½ pint) rum
600 ml (1 pint) boiling water

Rub the rind of the lemon with the loaf sugar. Put with all the remaining ingredients in a pan on the stove. Heat gently but do not let it boil. Squeeze the lemon juice and strain into a punch bowl. Pour the hot liquid on top and serve at once.

Mead

On the sixteenth of April, Ross had gone up to the mine and Demelza and Jinny and Jane were brewing mead. They were enjoying themselves. They had stirred six pounds of honey into a couple of gallons of warm water and added some dried elder flowers and ginger. This was on the fire to boil in a large pan, and Jane was skimming it with a spoon whenever a frothy scum formed on the surface.

Demelza, Book Two, Chapter IV

Elsewhere in Cornwall, mead was made from honey and grape juice. Liqueur mead had brandy added.

Elderflower Wine

1.2 l (2 pints) elderflowers
4 lemons
4 oranges
3.5 kg (8 lbs) brown sugar
100 g (4 oz) root ginger
9 l (2 gallons) boiling water
50 g (2 oz) wine yeast

Pick all the stalks off the flowers and put flowers into a large earthenware bowl. Slice all the fruit and add it with the sugar to the bowl. Put the ginger in a piece of muslin and add this. Cover with boiling water and leave to steep. When cool, add the yeast. Leave to stand for a few days, stirring daily. Strain and bottle. Store in a cool place.

Turnip Wine

This is a popular way of using some of the surfeit of turnips that used to abound.

———————※———————

Take as many turnips as you please. Pare and slice them, then put them into a cider press and press out all the juice. To every 4.5 l (1 gallon) of juice put 1.5 kg (3 lbs) lump sugar. Put together in a vessel just big enough to hold them (usually an old beer or brandy barrel was used). To every 4.5 litres (1 gallon) of juice add 300 ml (½ pint) of brandy. Cover the bung for a week and then close tight. Let it stand for three months and then draw off and put into bottles.

You will be surprised how much juice comes out of turnips, and as I have said before these are the yellow swedes not the white, peppery type.

Dr Choake's Milk Punch

To 20 quarts of Brandy, put the rind of thirty Seville Oranges and twenty-six Lemons; let them infuse for twelve hours, then strain the Brandy from the peels and put to it thirty quarts of water. Bring to the boil, then leave to cool. Add the juice of the thirty oranges and the twenty-six lemons, and fifteen pounds of fine sugar. Put in a cask, adding one quart of new milk, boiled but cooled, mix it well together and stop the cask close. Let it stand till it is fine, which will be in about six weeks, then bottle it. You may keep it many years. The older it is the better.

Clearly this is a recipe to be made with the cheap brandy of the eighteenth century which was not burdened with excise duty!

Sir Walter Raleigh Cordial

Sir Walter Raleigh was Lord Warden of the Stannaries (the tin courts), Lord Lieutenant of Cornwall, and was in charge of the defence of Cornwall and Devon, during the late sixteenth century.

———— ❧ ————

15 g (½ oz) yellow sanders (sandalwood)
15 g (½ oz) cinnamon
15 g (½ oz) cochineal
1.75 l (3 pints) brandy
450 g (1 lb) sugar

Pound the sandalwood, cinnamon and cochineal well and infuse them in the brandy. Stir this mixture every day for a fortnight.

Then take the sugar and boil it over a gentle fire in 1.75 l (3 pints) of spring water till it has reduced to 1.2 l (1 quart). When it is quite cold, strain the brandy and mix the syrup with it.

Small Beer

A beer of considerable strength brewed in Penryn in the sixteenth century was known locally as 'lift leg'.

A hogshead varied somewhat in capacity according to the locality and use. When applied, to beer, it was generally 245 l (54 gallons).

———— ☙ ————

TO MAKE A HALF HOGSHEAD
45 l (1¼ bushels) of malt
50 g (2 oz) best hops

Put the malt into a large pan or cauldron, and heat over a fire. Add the hops before it begins boiling. Keep simmering for 2 hours and then pour it off into the cooler. As soon as it comes to a head in the vat, turn it directly. It must stand open for 3 or 4 days and will be fit to drink in a fortnight.

Jud and Prudie's Tipple

Jud turned and looked at Prudie assessingly.

'Gis along, you. 'Ere, there's brandy in the cupboard. Fetch it down and I'll mix ee a Sampson.'

This had once been Prudie's favourite drink: brandy and cider and sugar. She stared at Jud as if he were the Devil tempting her to sell her soul.

She said: 'If I'd want drink I'll get it and not akse you, nor no other else.' She went to the cupboard and genteelly mixed herself a Sampson. With greedy, glassy eyes Jud watched her.

'Now,' said Prudie fiercely, 'out o' that chair!'

Jud wiped a hand across his face. 'Dear life, it d'make me weep to see ee. Drink un up first. An' mix me one too. Mix me a Sampson wi' his hair on. There, there, be a good wife, now.'

Demelza, Book One, Chapter XIII

A 'Sampson with his hair on' was the same drink but with double the brandy.

Bishop

MAKES 6 GLASSFULS

1 large orange
12 cloves
1 bottle of port
sugar

Stick the orange with the cloves. Put in a closely covered dish and roast in the oven until nice and brown. Cut into 8 pieces and remove pips. Gently heat the port and add pieces of orange to it. Sweeten to taste and simmer for 20 minutes – on no account must it boil. Strain and serve hot.

Mahogany

Mix together 1 part treacle to 2 parts of gin.

On Friday March 30 I dined with him at Sir Joshua Reynolds', with the Earl of Charlemont, Sir Annesley Stewart, Mr Eliot of Port Eliot, Mr Burke, Dean Morlay, Mr Langton; a most agreeable day, of which I regret every circumstance is not preserved; but it is unreasonable to require such a multiplication of felicity . . .

Mr Eliot mentioned a curious liquor peculiar to his county, which the Cornish fishermen drink. They call it *Mahogany*; and it is made of two parts gin and one part treacle, well beaten together. I begged to have some of it made, which was done with proper skill by Mr Eliot. I thought it very good liquor, and said it was a counterpart of what is called *Athol Porridge* in the Highlands of Scotland, which is a mixture of whisky and honey. Johnson said: 'That must be a better liquor than the Cornish, for both its component parts are better.' He also observed: '*Mahogany* must be a modern name; for it is not long since the wood called mahogany was known in this country.' A variation of Mahogany was served at Julia's christening (*Demelza*, Book One, Chapter V). 'When the party began to break up . . . Ross had them all served with a stiff glass of brandy and treacle.'

Boswell's Life of Johnson, 30 March, 1781

We had a very elegant dinner. The first course was part of a large Cod, a Chine of Mutton, some Soup, a Chicken Pye, Puddings and Roots. Second course, Pidgeons and Asparagus, A Filet of Veal with Mushrooms and high sauce, rosted Sweetbreads, hot Lobster, Apricot Tart and in the middle a Pyramid of Syllabubs and Jellies. We had a Desert of Fruit after Dinner, and Madeira, white Port and red to drink as Wine. We were all very cheerful and merry.

Entry in Parson Woodforde's
diary for April 20, 1774

Dinner today rost Beef, plumb Pudding and Mince Pies. Six poor people dined at my House, and after I gave them 1/-, I burnt for one Hour this evening my old Wax Candle, as usual on this High-day. It is almost finished, it might last for once more, and that is all it can do.

Entry in Parson Woodforde's diary for
Christmas Day, a quarter of a century later

Index

Aberdeen Sausage 58
Almond Cake 119–20
Almond Custard 50
Apple Frazes 189
Apple Fritters 188
Apricot Tart 154
Asparagus 151

Batter Pudding 101
Beef, Boiled 127
Beef Pie 69
Beef, Roast 148
Beetroot, Pickled 164
Bee Wine 76
Biscuits, Wine or Sweet
    185
Bishop 207
Black Caps 104
Blancmange 105
Bombay Duck 59
Brawn 61
Bread 113–15

Capon, Roast 71
Chervil Tart 190
Christening Cake 72
Christmas Cake 50
Chutney 165
Cod, Boiled 147
Conger Eel Pie 81
Consommé 19–20
Cornish Cream 179
Cow Heel Soup 16
Cressey Supe 22
Custard 104

Damson Cheese 184
Damson Tart 103
Duck 150

Egg and Bacon Pie 87
Elderflower Wine 201

Figgy 'Obbin 187
Figs, Preserved 168
Fish Pie 31

Fowl, Boiled 99
Fowl Pie 82–3
Friar's Omelet 183

Giblet Pie 91
Gingerbread 75
Gooseberry Preserve 167
Goose, Roast 70–1
Gravy 63
Grey Mullet 34

Ham 99
Heavy Cake 73
Hen Turkey 175
Herrings, Baked 37–8
Herrings, Fried 37
Hog's Pudding 60

Jelly 186
Jud and Prudie's Tipple
    206

Lamb Tail Pie 85
Lardy Bread 116
Leek Pasty 137–8
Lemon Meringue Pie 193–4
Lemon Pudding 156
Lentil Soup 21

Mackerel, Marinated 36
Mackerel with Gooseberry Sauce
    32–3
Mahogany 208–9
Marrow 62
Mead 200
Meat and Potato Pasty 135–6

Meat and Potato Pie 86
Milk Punch 203
Minced Beef Pasty 139
Mincemeat 92–3
Mince Pies 49
Mushrooms 151
Mutton, Boiled 100
Mutton, Hashed 55
Mutton Steaks 44

Natlings 57
Nettle Soup 15

Orange Pudding 148–9
Oxtail Soup 17–18

Parsley Pasty 140
Partridge Pie 45
Pastry, Rough Puff 141
Pastry, Shortcrust 155
Pastry, Suet 149
Patties, Fried 88
Pea Soup 173
Pigeons 84
Pilchards, Baked 34
Plaice, Fried 35
Plum Cake 121–2
Plum Pudding 129–30
Poldark Trifle 191–2
Punch 199

Quince, Preserved 166

Rabbit, Fried 128
Raspbery Puffs 178
Red Currant Jelly 102

Red Gooseberry Preserve 167
Red Mullet 34

Saffron Cake 74
Salmon, Baked 36
Salmon, Boiled 35
Salmon, Pickled 38
Sampson 206
Sauce
    Brandy 48
    Bread 162
    Caper 100
    Cranberry 163
    Egg 162
    Gooseberry 32–3
        for Goose 71
    High (for Veal) 153–4
    Oyster 147
    Sorrel 164
    Sweet 43
    White 161
Sir Walter Raleigh Cordial 204
Skate 37
Small Beer 205

Snipe, Roast 46
Spinach Tart 190
Splits 111–12
Squab Pie 89
Starry-Gazy Pie 90
Stuffing
    Chestnut 176
    Sage 62
    Veal 177
Swan, Roast 43
Sweet Egg Pie 130
Syllabub 180

Tongue, Boiled 174
Turkey 127, 175
Turkey with Ham 127
Turnip and Potato Pasty 139
Turnip Wine 202

Underground Roast 56

Veal, Fricandeau of 152

Yeast Cake 117–18